Fascinating Facts & True Stories

of 45 People Who Shaped the World

WonderLab

First Print: 2025

Staten House ISBN **979-8-89860-106-5**

Table of Contents

INTRODUCTION

Have you ever wondered who built the world we live in today? Not with bricks and concrete—but with ideas, courage, creativity, and sometimes... a little rebellion.

This book is your time machine.

Inside, you'll discover 45 fascinating people from all around the globe who changed history in their own unique way. Some were scientists. Others were explorers, inventors, artists, or leaders. A few were quiet thinkers. Others made a lot of noise. But all of them made a difference.

You'll find **facts**—surprising, weird, and wow-worthy. And behind each fact, there's a **reason**: a "why" that helps you

These stories aren't just about the past.
They'll help you understand the present—and maybe even inspire you to shape the future.

So, turn the page.

History isn't just something you read about.

It's full of real people. Real facts. And stories you'll never for-get.

George Washington

Born: 1732 – *Died:* 1799

Country: United States

Known for: First President of the United States, General in the American Revolutionary War

Fun Fact: He never lived in the White House!

George Washington helped create a new country—and then led it as its very first president. Long before his face appeared on the dollar bill, he was a land surveyor, a general, and a man admired for his honesty and leadership.

Fascinating Facts & Why They Matter

❖ **Fact:** George Washington was the first President of the United States.
Why? He was elected in 1789 and served two terms until 1797. Many of the things American presidents do today—like serving only two terms—started with him.

❖ **Fact:** He never lived in the White House.
Why? The White House wasn't finished yet! During his presidency, Washington lived in official residences in New York City and Philadelphia.

❖ **Fact:** His teeth weren't made of wood.
Why? That's just a myth. His dentures were made from a mix of materials—including human teeth, animal teeth, and ivory. Not very comfortable!

❖ **Fact:** Before becoming a general, he worked as a land surveyor.
Why? This early job taught him how to read and map land—skills that helped him during battles in the Revolutionary War.

❖ **Fact:** Washington led the Continental Army to victory in the American Revolution.
Why? His leadership helped defeat the British, leading

to American independence. Without him, the United States might not even exist today.

* **Fact:** He was unanimously elected president.
  Why? Every elector voted for him—twice! He was that respected by the people.

* **Fact:** Washington loved dogs.
  Why? He owned many and even bred hunting dogs. Some of their names? Sweet Lips, Vulcan, and Drunkard!

* **Fact:** He was one of the wealthiest men in America at the time.
  Why? He owned Mount Vernon, a large plantation where crops like wheat and tobacco were grown and sold.

* **Fact:** Washington was famous for his honesty.
  Why? Tales like the cherry tree story—whether true or not—reflect how people saw him: trustworthy and fair.

* **Fact:** He started the tradition of a farewell address.
  Why? When he left the office, Washington gave a speech to guide the country's future. Presidents still follow that tradition today.

Cleopatra

Born: 69 BCE – **Died:** 30 BCE
Country: Egypt
Known for: Last pharaoh of Ancient Egypt, political strategist, and symbol of female power
Fun Fact: She spoke at least seven languages!

Cleopatra wasn't just a queen—she was a clever ruler, a skilled negotiator, and a bold leader who stood toe to toe with the most powerful men of her time. Her story is filled with power, politics, and mystery, making her one of the most unforgettable figures in history.

Fascinating Facts & Why They Matter

❖ **Fact:** Cleopatra was the last pharaoh of Ancient Egypt. **Why?** After her death, Egypt became a Roman province. She ruled during the final days of Egypt's independence and fought to keep her kingdom strong.

❖ **Fact:** She was not Egyptian by blood. **Why?** Cleopatra belonged to the Ptolemaic dynasty, a family of Greek origin that ruled Egypt after Alexander the Great's empire split. She was the first of her family to speak Egyptian fluently.

❖ **Fact:** Cleopatra spoke many languages. **Why?** Historians believe she spoke at least seven languages. This helped her communicate with leaders across different regions and made her a powerful diplomat.

❖ **Fact:** She met two of the most famous Roman leaders: Julius Caesar and Mark Antony. **Why?** Cleopatra formed political and personal alliances with both men to protect Egypt and her throne. These relationships changed the course of Roman history.

❖ **Fact:** Cleopatra was highly educated. **Why?** She studied philosophy, mathematics, astronomy, and more. In a time when many women had little access to education, she stood out as a brilliant mind.

❖ **Fact:** Cleopatra used her image carefully. **Why?** She presented herself as the goddess Isis to strengthen her authority and inspire loyalty from the Egyptian people.

❖ **Fact:** Her life inspired many stories, plays, and films. **Why?** Cleopatra's dramatic life, beauty, and political power made her a fascinating figure for writers and artists across centuries—including Shakespeare!

❖ **Fact:** Cleopatra died by suicide at age 39. **Why?** Facing defeat by Rome, she is said to have taken her own life—possibly using a poisonous snake called an asp. Her death marked the end of Ancient Egypt's great era.

Leonardo da Vinci

Born: 1452 – **Died:** 1519
Country: Italy
Known for: Painter, inventor, scientist, and one of the greatest minds of the Renaissance
Fun Fact: He often wrote backwards—his notes could only be read in a mirror!

Leonardo da Vinci wasn't just a painter—he was a thinker, an explorer of ideas, and a genius ahead of his time. From flying machines to famous artworks, he turned curiosity into creativity and left a mark on the world that still inspires people today.

Fascinating Facts & Why They Matter

❖ **Fact:** Leonardo was a master of many trades. **Why?** He wasn't only a brilliant painter, but also an inventor, scientist, engineer, and musician. That's why people call him a true "Renaissance man"—someone skilled in many areas.

❖ **Fact:** He painted the famous *Mona Lisa*. **Why?** Known for her mysterious smile, this portrait is one of the most famous paintings in the world and still attracts millions of visitors to the Louvre Museum in Paris.

❖ **Fact:** *The Last Supper* is one of his masterpieces. **Why?** He used a technique called linear perspective to create a sense of depth, making the scene look almost three-dimensional—a big deal at the time!

❖ **Fact:** Leonardo was fascinated by flight. **Why?** Long before airplanes, he studied birds and sketched flying machines, including a design for a helicopter-like device, centuries before airplanes were invented.

❖ **Fact:** He wrote in reverse.
Why? His notes often used mirror writing. Some think it was to keep his ideas secret, while others say it was simply more comfortable for him as a left-handed writer.

❖ **Fact:** His notebooks were full of inventions.
Why? He imagined things like tanks, diving suits, and even mechanical lions—centuries before they could be built. His creativity was limitless.

❖ **Fact:** He studied the human body in great detail.
Why? By dissecting cadavers, Leonardo learned how muscles and bones worked. This helped him make more accurate art and advanced early medical knowledge.

❖ **Fact:** He drew the famous *Vitruvian Man*.
Why? This drawing shows how the human body fits into both a circle and a square, symbolizing the connection between math, science, and art.

❖ **Fact:** Leonardo was left-handed.
Why? Left-handedness was rare and sometimes discouraged, but it may have given him a unique way of seeing and expressing the world.

❖ **Fact:** His influence reached far beyond his lifetime. **Why?** Artists, scientists, and engineers still study his work today. His imagination helped shape the modern world.

Joan of Arc

Born: 1412 – **Died:** 1431
Country: France
Known for: Leading the French army during the Hundred Years' War and becoming a national heroine
Fun Fact: She led soldiers into battle at just 17 years old!

Joan of Arc was a teenage girl with no army training, yet she became one of France's greatest heroes. Guided by her faith and determination, she wore armor, led troops into battle, and changed the course of history—all before her 20th birthday.

Fascinating Facts & Why They Matter

❖ **Fact:** Joan of Arc led the French army to victory at age 17. **Why?** She believed she was sent by God to help France defeat the English in the Hundred Years' War. Her bravery inspired the troops and helped turn the tide of the war.

❖ **Fact:** She was born a peasant girl. **Why?** Joan came from a small village and had no formal education or military training. Her rise to leadership made her story even more extraordinary.

❖ **Fact:** Joan wore armor like a knight. **Why?** To lead soldiers into battle, she dressed in full armor and carried a banner instead of a sword. Her presence gave hope and courage to her troops.

❖ **Fact:** She was captured by enemy forces. **Why?** During a battle, Joan was taken prisoner and handed over to the English, who saw her as a threat to their power.

❖ **Fact:** Joan was put on trial for her beliefs. **Why?** The English accused her of heresy and witchcraft because she claimed to hear divine voices. The trial was unfair and meant to silence her.

❖ **Fact:** She died at just 19 years old. **Why?** Joan was burned at the stake, but her strength and faith turned her into a symbol of courage and sacrifice.

❖ **Fact:** She was declared a saint in 1920. **Why?** The Catholic Church officially recognized her bravery and holiness, making her one of the most famous saints in history.

❖ **Fact:** Her story has inspired millions. **Why?** Books, plays, and films have told her story over and over, celebrating her as a fearless leader and national icon.

❖ **Fact:** Her battle banner was white with lilies. **Why?** The banner showed her devotion and purity. It was decorated with religious symbols instead of weapons.

❖ **Fact:** France honors her every year. **Why?** May 30th, the day of her death, is a National Day of Remembrance in France. Joan remains a symbol of unity, strength, and faith.

Albert Einstein

Born: 1879 – **Died:** 1955
Country: Germany / later United States
Known for: Theories of relativity, Nobel Prize-winning physicist, symbol of scientific genius
Fun Fact: He didn't start speaking until he was about four years old!

Albert Einstein didn't talk much as a child, had wild hair, and hated socks—but he grew up to change how we understand the universe. His curious mind, love for music, and deep thoughts about time, space, and peace made him one of the greatest thinkers in history.

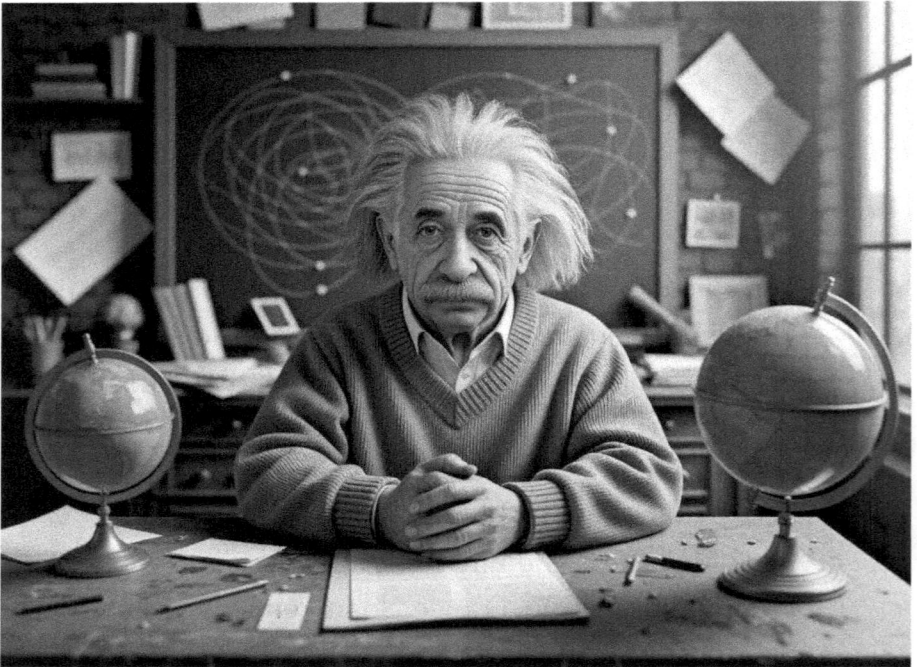

- ❖ **Fact:** Einstein was a late talker.
  Why? He didn't speak full sentences until around age four, which worried his parents. But his slow start didn't stop him from becoming one of the most brilliant minds ever.

- ❖ **Fact:** He loved playing the violin.
  Why? Music helped him relax and think. He often said that playing his violin gave him some of his best scientific ideas.

- ❖ **Fact:** His hair was famously wild.
  Why? He didn't care much about how he looked—his messy hair became part of his unique image and made him instantly recognizable.

- ❖ **Fact:** His theory of relativity changed physics.
  Why? It showed that time and space are connected. His famous formula, $E = mc^2$, explained how energy and mass are related—one of the most important ideas in science.

- ❖ **Fact:** He won the Nobel Prize in Physics in 1921.
  Why? He was honored for his work on the photoelectric

effect, which helped scientists understand how light and energy work at the smallest level.

- ❖ **Fact:** He was offered the presidency of Israel.
  Why? Even though he wasn't a politician, Israel's leaders respected him so much that they offered him the position in 1952. He politely declined, saying it wasn't the right fit.

- ❖ **Fact:** Einstein loved sailing.
  Why? He enjoyed the peace and quiet on the water, even though he wasn't a strong swimmer and often drifted off course!

- ❖ **Fact:** He had a famously messy desk.
  Why? He believed that a cluttered desk meant an active mind. He worked surrounded by papers, books, and ideas in progress.

- ❖ **Fact:** He was a pacifist.
  Why? Einstein believed in peace and spoke out against war. But during World War II, he supported the creation of the atomic bomb—hoping it would help end the fighting quickly.

- ❖ **Fact:** His brain was studied after his death.
  Why? Scientists wanted to discover what made him so intelligent. They preserved parts of his brain and studied its structure in search of clues.

Marie Curie

Born: 1867 - **Died;** 1934

Country: Poland / France

Known for: Pioneering research on radioactivity, first woman to win a Nobel Prize, and the only person to win Nobel Prizes in two sciences

Fun Fact: Her research notebooks are still radioactive!

Marie Curie didn't just make history—she changed science forever. As a physicist, chemist, teacher, and mother, she broke barriers and discovered elements that opened a whole new world of knowledge. And she did it all when few believed women could become scientists.

Fascinating Facts & Why They Matter

❖ **Fact:** Marie Curie was the first woman to win a Nobel Prize.
Why? In 1903, she received the Nobel Prize in Physics for her groundbreaking work on radioactivity—a word she invented!

❖ **Fact:** She's the only person to win Nobel Prizes in two different sciences.
Why? In 1911, she won the Nobel Prize in Chemistry for discovering two radioactive elements: radium and polonium.

❖ **Fact:** She was born in Poland.
Why? Marie was born in Warsaw, and later moved to France to study science, since women couldn't attend university in Poland at the time.

❖ **Fact:** She worked closely with her husband, Pierre Curie.
Why? Together, they made major discoveries in radioactivity and shared the 1903 Nobel Prize. They were true scientific partners.

❖ **Fact:** She named the element polonium after her home-land.
Why? Poland wasn't an independent country at the time, and naming the element was her way of honoring her roots.

❖ **Fact:** She worked in a very basic lab.
Why? Marie and Pierre's lab was an old shed with poor equipment—but that didn't stop them from changing science forever.

❖ **Fact:** She became the first female professor at the University of Paris.
Why? After Pierre's death, Marie took over his teaching position—becoming a trailblazer for women in education.

❖ **Fact:** Her research helped develop X-ray machines.
Why? The use of radioactive materials in medical imaging owes much to her work, especially in diagnosing injuries.

❖ **Fact:** She brought mobile X-ray units to World War I.
Why? She traveled to the front lines to help doctors treat wounded soldiers using portable X-ray technology she helped design.

❖ **Fact:** Her notebooks are still radioactive today. **Why?** Because she worked directly with radioactive substances, her papers must be handled with special protection—even now!

❖ **Fact:** She founded the Radium Institute in Paris. **Why?** This research center trained future scientists and continued her mission to explore radioactivity and its uses.

❖ **Fact:** Her daughter also won a Nobel Prize. **Why?** Irène Joliot-Curie, with her husband Frédéric, continued Marie's work and won the Nobel Prize in Chemistry in 1935.

❖ **Fact:** She received many honorary degrees. **Why?** Universities around the world recognized her incredible contributions to science and education.

❖ **Fact:** Her legacy continues to inspire. **Why?** Marie Curie's courage, curiosity, and brilliance make her a role model for scientists—especially young women—around the globe.

Martin Luther King Jr.

Born: 1929 – **Died:** 1968
Country: United States
Known for: Civil rights leader, Nobel Peace Prize winner, and symbol of nonviolent resistance
Fun Fact: He entered college at just 15 years old!

Martin Luther King Jr. believed that the world could change—not through violence, but through peace, courage, and powerful words. As a pastor, writer, and leader, he stood up for justice and equality, inspiring millions to dream of a better future.

Fascinating Facts & Why They Matter

❖ **Fact:** Martin Luther King Jr. was a gifted speaker. **Why?** He gave over 2,500 speeches during his life. His words were so powerful that they moved people to take action for change.

❖ **Fact:** He skipped two grades in school. **Why?** He was so advanced that he jumped from ninth to eleventh grade and entered college at just 15—a sign of his incredible intelligence and focus.

❖ **Fact:** He won the Nobel Peace Prize in 1964. **Why?** His peaceful fight against racism and segregation earned him the world's highest honor for promoting peace and human rights.

❖ **Fact:** He led the Montgomery Bus Boycott. **Why?** After Rosa Parks refused to give up her seat to a white passenger, King helped organize a peaceful protest that lasted 381 days—and led to a major victory for civil rights.

❖ **Fact:** He had a dream.
Why? In his famous 1963 "I Have a Dream" speech, he

imagined a world where people would be judged by their character, not the color of their skin. That speech still inspires people today.

❖ **Fact:** He was inspired by Mahatma Gandhi. **Why?** King admired Gandhi's idea of using nonviolence to create change. He used similar peaceful methods in protests, marches, and speeches.

❖ **Fact:** He was arrested 29 times. **Why?** He broke unfair laws through peaceful protest. Even when jailed, he never gave up on his mission to bring justice to all.

❖ **Fact:** He was a pastor. **Why?** King became a minister at 19 and used his church as a platform to speak out against racism and injustice.

❖ **Fact:** Martin Luther King Jr. Day is a national holiday. **Why?** Celebrated every third Monday in January, this day honors his life, his message, and his lasting impact on the fight for equality.

❖ **Fact:** He was also a talented writer. **Why?** Through books and articles, King shared his vision of a fair society. His words continue to teach and inspire people around the world.

Amelia Earhart

Born: 1897 – **Disappeared:** 1937
Country: United States
Known for: Aviation pioneer, first woman to fly solo across the Atlantic, and symbol of fearless exploration
Fun Fact: Her first airplane was bright yellow and nicknamed "The Canary"!

Amelia Earhart was more than a pilot—she was a record-breaker, adventurer, and fearless trailblazer. From flying across oceans to designing clothes and teaching young women, she proved that the sky was never the limit.

Fascinating Facts & Why They Matter

❖ **Fact:** She was the first woman to fly solo across the Atlantic Ocean.
Why? In 1932, Amelia flew alone from Newfoundland, Canada, to Ireland in about 15 hours, becoming a global icon for courage and skill.

❖ **Fact:** She set a world altitude record for female pilots.
Why? In 1931, she flew up to 18,415 feet—a new height record for women pilots at the time.

❖ **Fact:** She was the first person to fly solo from Hawaii to California.
Why? In 1935, she completed the 2,408-mile flight, showing that long-distance air travel over the ocean was possible—even alone.

❖ **Fact:** Amelia was a best-selling author.
Why? She wrote books about her flying adventures that inspired readers around the world, especially girls who dreamed big.

❖ **Fact:** She was a fashion designer.
Why? She created stylish yet practical clothes for active

women—perfect for flying, exploring, or simply standing out.

❖ **Fact:** She helped found The Ninety-Nines. **Why?** This group supported women in aviation. Amelia believed that women pilots should help one another succeed.

❖ **Fact:** She received the Distinguished Flying Cross. **Why?** This military honor was awarded for her solo Atlantic flight—an incredible feat of bravery and precision.

❖ **Fact:** She volunteered as a nurse's aide during World War I.
Why? Amelia cared for wounded soldiers in Canada before becoming a pilot, showing her dedication to helping others.

❖ **Fact:** Her first plane was called "The Canary." **Why?** It was bright yellow, and she used it to set early flying records—including a women's altitude record.

❖ **Fact:** She disappeared during an attempt to fly around the world.
Why? In 1937, Amelia vanished over the Pacific Ocean.

Despite search efforts, her plane was never found, leaving behind a lasting mystery.

❖ **Fact:** She worked as a social worker. **Why?** Before becoming famous, she helped immigrants and struggling families in Boston, showing her compassion and leadership.

❖ **Fact:** She was the first woman to receive the National Geographic Society's Gold Medal. **Why?** She was honored for her daring flights and her role in advancing exploration.

❖ **Fact:** She taught aviation at Purdue University. **Why?** Amelia encouraged young women to pursue science, engineering, and flying—fields that were mostly male-dominated at the time.

❖ **Fact:** Her nickname was "Lady Lindy." **Why?** People compared her to Charles Lindbergh, who also made a solo Atlantic flight. Her courage and success earned her the title.

❖ **Fact:** Her legacy still inspires people today. **Why?** Amelia showed that with passion and courage, anyone can reach for the sky—and beyond.

Mahatma Gandhi

Born: 1869 – **Died:** 1948
Country: India
Known for: Leader of India's independence movement, champion of nonviolent resistance
Fun Fact: He walked 240 miles during the Salt March to protest unfair laws!

Mahatma Gandhi believed that true strength comes from peace, not violence. Through simple living and powerful ideas, he helped lead India to freedom and inspired peaceful movements all over the world.

* **Fact:** Gandhi was a lawyer.
  Why? He studied law in London and became a barrister. His legal training helped him speak out for justice and organize peaceful protests.

* **Fact:** He led the Salt March.
  Why? In 1930, Gandhi marched 240 miles to protest the British tax on salt. The peaceful protest inspired thousands to join him and became a turning point in India's struggle for independence.

* **Fact:** He believed in nonviolent protest.
  Why? Gandhi followed the principle of **ahimsa**, meaning nonviolence. He showed that peaceful resistance could be stronger than weapons.

* **Fact:** He was lovingly called "Bapu."
  Why? "Bapu" means "father" in Gujarati, and many people called him the Father of the Nation for his role in India's freedom movement.

* **Fact:** He used fasting as a protest.
  Why? Gandhi would stop eating to protest violence and

injustice. His fasts made people stop and reflect, often bringing peace during difficult times.

- ❖ **Fact:** He was inspired by the *Bhagavad Gita*. **Why?** This ancient Hindu text shaped his beliefs in truth, self-discipline, and nonviolence.

- ❖ **Fact:** He was nominated for the Nobel Peace Prize five times.
  Why? His peaceful methods earned him global respect, but surprisingly, he never received the award.

- ❖ **Fact:** He wore very simple clothes.
  Why? Gandhi chose to wear a hand-spun dhoti to show support for India's poor and to promote self-reliance.

- ❖ **Fact:** His birthday is a national holiday in India.
  Why? October 2nd is celebrated as *Gandhi Jayanti*, a day to remember his message of peace and freedom.

- ❖ **Fact:** His teachings inspired movements around the world.
  Why? Leaders like Martin Luther King Jr. and Nelson Mandela used Gandhi's nonviolent methods in their own fights for justice.

Queen Elisabeth I

Born: 1533 – **Died:** 1603
Country: England
Known for: Queen of England for 45 years, symbol of power and independence during the Elizabethan Era
Fun Fact: She had over 2,000 dresses in her royal wardrobe!

Queen Elizabeth I ruled with strength, intelligence, and flair. Refusing to marry, she led England through a golden age of exploration, culture, and political power—earning her a place as one of the most iconic monarchs in history.

❖ Fascinating Facts & Why They Matter

- ❖ **Fact:** She was known as the "Virgin Queen." **Why?** Elizabeth never married. She chose to remain single to keep full control over her kingdom and avoid sharing power with a king.

- ❖ **Fact:** She reigned for 45 years. **Why?** Her rule, from 1558 to 1603, brought stability and growth to England. This time is now known as the *Elizabethan Era*, famous for its culture and progress.

- ❖ **Fact:** She loved fashion and owned over 2,000 dresses. **Why?** Her elaborate gowns and jewels weren't just for show—they were a way to display her wealth, status, and royal authority.

- ❖ **Fact:** She survived smallpox. **Why?** In 1562, Elizabeth became seriously ill but recovered. Though she was left with scars, she continued to appear in public, often wearing white makeup to cover them.

- ❖ **Fact:** She supported the arts. **Why?** Elizabeth was a major patron of writers and performers. Her support helped talents like William Shakespeare rise to fame.

❖ **Fact:** She defeated the Spanish Armada. **Why?** In 1588, England's navy beat the powerful Spanish fleet. It was a huge victory that protected England's independence and made Elizabeth a national hero.

❖ **Fact:** She spoke several languages. **Why?** Elizabeth was fluent in Latin, French, Italian, Spanish, and, of course, English—making her a strong and skillful ruler in diplomacy.

❖ **Fact:** Her mother was Anne Boleyn. **Why?** Anne was King Henry VIII's second wife. Elizabeth's birth and later rise to power were deeply tied to the famous Tudor family drama.

❖ **Fact:** She was once imprisoned in the Tower of London. **Why?** Before becoming queen, Elizabeth was suspected of plotting against her sister, Queen Mary I, and was locked in the Tower. She survived—and later became
❖ queen herself.

❖ **Fact:** Her reign encouraged exploration. **Why?** Under her rule, explorers like Sir Francis Drake and

Sir Walter Raleigh sailed the world, expanding England's global influence.

* **Fact:** She gave a famous speech at Tilbury. **Why?** Before the battle against the Spanish Armada, Elizabeth addressed her troops, saying she had "the heart and stomach of a king"—and won their loyalty.

* **Fact:** Her royal symbol was the Tudor Rose. **Why?** The rose stood for the unity of two rival royal families, symbolizing peace and strength in her rule.

* **Fact:** She reinforced the Church of England. **Why?** Elizabeth supported Protestantism, continuing her father's break from the Catholic Church and shaping England's religious future.

* **Fact:** Her nickname was "Gloriana." **Why?** This poetic name celebrated her as a glorious and triumphant monarch during one of England's brightest eras.

* **Fact:** Her portraits were full of symbols. **Why?** Artists painted her with crowns, globes, and other icons to show her power, wisdom, and royal image.

Thomas Edison

Born: 1847 – **Died:** 1931
Country: United States
Known for: Inventor of the phonograph, motion picture camera, and improved light bulb
Fun Fact: He held over 1,000 patents in his lifetime!

Thomas Edison turned imagination into invention. From sound recordings to electric light, his work helped shape the modern world. He never stopped experimenting—and believed that hard work and curiosity were the keys to success.

Fascinating Facts & Why They Matter

❖ **Fact:** He had over 1,000 patents. **Why?** Edison invented or improved many devices, from the electric light bulb to early movie cameras. He was one of the most productive inventors in history.

❖ **Fact:** He was called the "Wizard of Menlo Park." **Why?** His laboratory in Menlo Park, New Jersey, became famous for constant innovation. People saw him as a kind of genius inventor—or wizard!

❖ **Fact:** He invented the phonograph. **Why?** In 1877, Edison created the first machine that could record and play back sound—something no one had ever done before.

❖ **Fact:** He improved the electric light bulb. **Why?** He didn't invent the very first bulb, but he made one that was practical, long-lasting, and safe for everyday use.

❖ **Fact:** He started the first industrial research lab. **Why?** Edison built a team of inventors to work together on new ideas. It was the first time invention was organized like a business.

❖ **Fact:** He was partially deaf.
Why? He lost most of his hearing as a child. Instead of seeing it as a problem, Edison said it helped him focus without distractions.

❖ **Fact:** He invented the motion picture camera.
Why? He created the *Kinetoscope*, one of the first devices that let people watch moving pictures—an early step toward the movies we love today.

❖ **Fact:** He held a world record for patents.
Why? With 1,093 patents, Edison once held the record for the most inventions officially registered to one person.

❖ **Fact:** He created the first power station.
Why? In 1882, his *Pearl Street Station* began supplying electricity to homes and businesses in New York City, launching the modern power grid.

❖ **Fact:** He was a self-taught inventor.
Why? Edison had only a few months of formal schooling. He learned by reading, experimenting, and asking questions—showing that passion can be more powerful than a classroom.

Harriet Tubman

Born: 1822 – **Died:** 1913
Country: United States
Known for: Abolitionist, Underground Railroad conductor, Civil War spy, and women's rights activist
Fun Fact: She was nicknamed "Moses" for leading people to freedom!

Harriet Tubman risked everything for freedom—not just her own, but for dozens of others. Born into slavery, she became one of the most fearless conductors of the Underground Railroad and later a spy, nurse, and activist. Her courage lit the way for generations to come.

Fascinating Facts & Why They Matter

- ❖ **Fact:** She was called "Moses."
  Why? Like the biblical leader, Harriet led over 70 enslaved people to freedom through secret escape routes known as the Underground Railroad.

- ❖ **Fact:** She was born into slavery.
  Why? Born in Maryland around 1822, she escaped in 1849 and vowed to help others do the same.

- ❖ **Fact:** She never lost a passenger.
  Why? Harriet's missions were dangerous, but thanks to her careful planning and bravery, everyone she guided reached freedom safely.

- ❖ **Fact:** She worked as a spy during the Civil War.
  Why? Harriet gathered valuable information for the Union Army that helped them win battles—and helped free more enslaved people.

- ❖ **Fact:** She led an armed raid.
  Why? In the Combahee River Raid of 1863, she became the first woman to lead a military operation in U.S. history, rescuing over 700 enslaved people.

❖ **Fact:** She suffered a head injury as a child. **Why?** After being hit by heavy weights, she experienced seizures and visions, which she said guided her throughout her life.

❖ **Fact:** She served as a nurse in the war. **Why?** Using her knowledge of herbal medicine, Harriet cared for wounded soldiers and the sick during the Civil War.

❖ **Fact:** She helped plan the raid on Harper's Ferry. **Why?** Though she couldn't join the raid, she worked with abolitionist John Brown, who shared her fight for justice.

❖ **Fact:** She fought for women's rights. **Why?** After the war, Harriet became a suffragist, speaking at rallies to support women's right to vote.

❖ **Fact:** She was chosen for U.S. currency. **Why?** Plans were announced to place Harriet on the $20 bill as a tribute to her incredible role in American history.

❖ **Fact:** She lived to be over 90 years old. **Why?** Harriet died in 1913, having spent her long life fighting for freedom, justice, and equality.

- ❖ **Fact:** She adopted a daughter.
  Why? With her second husband, Nelson Davis, she adopted a girl named Gertie, building a family alongside her activism.

- ❖ **Fact:** She was illiterate.
  Why? Though she never learned to read or write, Harriet had an extraordinary memory and intelligence that guided her through dangerous missions.

- ❖ **Fact:** She received a military pension.
  Why? For her work as a nurse, scout, and spy during the Civil War, Harriet earned official recognition and a pension from the U.S. government.

- ❖ **Fact:** She founded a home for the elderly.
  Why? In her later years, she opened the Harriet Tubman Home for Aged and Indigent Negroes, continuing her mission to care for others until the very end.

Alexander the Great

Born: 356 BCE – **Died:** 323 BCE

Country: Ancient Macedonia (now part of Greece)

Known for: Conquering one of the largest empires in history, undefeated in battle, and spreading Greek culture

Fun Fact: He named more than 20 cities after himself—most called "Alexandria"!

Alexander the Great became king at just 20 years old—and changed the world. With bold strategies, fearless leadership, and a love of learning, he built an empire that stretched across three continents before the age of 33.

Fascinating Facts & Why They Matter

❖ **Fact:** He never lost a battle.
   Why? Alexander was a brilliant military strategist. His tactics and leadership led to victories in every battle he fought—even when outnumbered.

❖ **Fact:** He became king at age 20.
   Why? After his father, King Philip II, was assassinated, Alexander took the throne and immediately began expanding his empire.

❖ **Fact:** He created one of the largest empires in history.
   Why? By age 30, Alexander had conquered land from Greece to Egypt and India, building a vast empire unlike anything the world had seen.

❖ **Fact:** He named over 20 cities after himself.
   Why? He wanted to leave a legacy, so he founded many cities called *Alexandria*, including the famous one in Egypt.

❖ **Fact:** He was tutored by Aristotle.
   Why? His father hired the great philosopher to teach him

about science, philosophy, and leadership—shaping Alexander into a brilliant thinker.

❖ **Fact:** He tamed a wild horse named Bucephalus. **Why?** Alexander noticed the horse was afraid of its shadow. By turning it toward the sun, he calmed it and gained a loyal companion for life.

❖ **Fact:** He spread Greek culture across his empire. **Why?** Alexander encouraged the mix of Greek and local traditions, creating the *Hellenistic Era*, a time of cultural blending and growth.

❖ **Fact:** He was declared a god in Egypt. **Why?** Egyptians saw him as a liberator and honored him as both a pharaoh and a deity.

❖ **Fact:** His empire fell apart after his death. **Why?** Without naming a clear successor, his generals fought for power, eventually dividing the empire into separate kingdoms.

❖ **Fact:** His body was preserved in honey. **Why?** Honey was used to prevent decay. His body was displayed in a glass coffin in Alexandria after his death.

- ❖ **Fact:** His favorite book was the *Iliad*. **Why?** Alexander admired the Greek hero Achilles and carried a copy of the epic poem with him during his military campaigns.

- ❖ **Fact:** He founded the city of Alexandria in Egypt. **Why?** He wanted to create a center for learning and culture. Alexandria later became one of the most important cities in the ancient world.

- ❖ **Fact:** He used elephants in battle. **Why?** After encountering war elephants in India, he added them to his army as powerful and intimidating weapons.

- ❖ **Fact:** His mother claimed he was the son of Zeus. **Why?** She believed he was destined for greatness and wanted to strengthen his image as a divine ruler.

- ❖ **Fact:** His empire was divided after his death. **Why?** His top generals, called the *Diadochi*, split the empire into three main parts, leading to the rise of new kingdoms.

Rosa Parks

Born: 1913 – **Died:** 2005
Country: United States
Known for: Sparked the Montgomery Bus Boycott and became a symbol of the Civil Rights Movement
Fun Fact: Her quiet act of defiance lasted just a few seconds—but helped change a nation.

Rosa Parks wasn't loud or famous when she made her stand—she was simply tired of unfairness. With courage and dignity, she helped ignite a movement that brought down segregation and inspired generations to stand up for justice.

REALISTIC SUBECT

❖ **Fact:** She is known as the "Mother of the Civil Rights Movement."
Why? In 1955, Rosa refused to give up her bus seat to a white passenger. Her arrest sparked the Montgomery Bus Boycott, a key moment in the fight for equality.

❖ **Fact:** She was arrested for her act of defiance.
Why? By breaking segregation laws in Alabama, Rosa was jailed—but her brave stand gained national attention.

❖ **Fact:** She wasn't the first to resist bus segregation.
Why? Others like Claudette Colvin also protested, but Rosa's case gained widespread support and helped unify the movement.

❖ **Fact:** She worked as a seamstress.
Why? Before becoming a civil rights icon, Rosa worked in a department store tailoring clothes, living an ordinary life in Montgomery.

❖ **Fact:** She was a secretary for the NAACP.
Why? Rosa was already active in the civil rights move-

ment, working to investigate and fight against racial injustice.

❖ **Fact:** She received the Presidential Medal of Freedom. **Why?** In 1996, President Bill Clinton awarded her this high honor for her courage and lifelong commitment to equality.

❖ **Fact:** Her decision to stay seated lasted only a few seconds.
Why? That brief moment became a powerful act of resistance, proving how small actions can have a huge impact.

❖ **Fact:** Her arrest led to a 381-day bus boycott. **Why?** Montgomery's Black community refused to ride the buses until segregation was overturned—showing the power of peaceful protest.

❖ **Fact:** Her case reached the Supreme Court. **Why?** The Court ruled that bus segregation was unconstitutional, helping end racist laws on public transportation.

❖ **Fact:** She wrote an autobiography. **Why?** In *Rosa Parks: My Story*, she shared her life and the events that led to her historic stand.

❖ **Fact:** She was born in Tuskegee, Alabama. **Why?** This town had a strong African American cultural legacy that shaped Rosa's early life.

❖ **Fact:** She moved to Detroit after the boycott. **Why?** Seeking better opportunities, she and her husband continued their activism in Michigan.

❖ **Fact:** She was honored with a statue in the U.S. Capitol. **Why?** In 2013, she became the first African American woman to be recognized with a statue in the Capitol building.

❖ **Fact:** She received the Congressional Gold Medal. **Why?** In 1999, she was awarded this prestigious honor for her unwavering fight for justice.

❖ **Fact:** Her legacy continues to inspire. **Why?** Rosa's quiet strength reminds us all that courage doesn't have to be loud—it just has to be true.

Julius Caesar

Born: 100 BCE – **Died:** 44 BCE
Country: Ancient Rome
Known for: Roman general, statesman, writer, and key figure in the fall of the Roman Republic
Fun Fact: He was once kidnapped by pirates—and told them they weren't asking enough ransom!

Julius Caesar was a fearless general, a gifted speaker, and a master of politics. From leading armies across Europe to re-forming Roman laws, his choices shaped the future of Rome—and still echo through history today.

Fascinating Facts & Why They Matter

❖ **Fact:** He was kidnapped by pirates. **Why?** At age 25, pirates captured him and demanded ransom. Caesar joked they should ask for more—because he was worth it! After being freed, he hunted them down.

❖ **Fact:** He was a brilliant military leader. **Why?** Caesar conquered Gaul (modern-day France and Belgium), expanding Rome's territory and gaining huge popularity.

❖ **Fact:** He was the first Roman to invade Britain. **Why?** In 55 BCE, he led two expeditions to Britain, opening contact between Rome and the British Isles for the first time.

❖ **Fact:** He was a great writer. **Why?** Caesar wrote clear, vivid accounts of his military campaigns, especially *The Gallic Wars*. These texts are still studied for their style and detail.

❖ **Fact:** He changed the calendar. **Why?** He introduced the **Julian calendar**, with 365 days and leap years. It's the basis of the calendar we still use today!

❖ **Fact:** He was declared "dictator for life." **Why?** In 44 BCE, the Roman Senate gave him full control of the government—a move that worried many and led to his downfall.

❖ **Fact:** He was assassinated on the Ides of March. **Why?** On March 15, 44 BCE, a group of senators stabbed him 23 times, fearing he was becoming too powerful.

❖ **Fact:** His death ended the Roman Republic. **Why?** Caesar's assassination caused civil wars that ended the Republic and gave rise to the Roman Empire, led by his adopted heir, Augustus.

❖ **Fact:** He was popular with the people. **Why?** Caesar introduced reforms to help the poor, including giving land and food. Many Romans admired his leadership.

❖ **Fact:** His name became a title. **Why?** "Caesar" became a symbol of power. Future emperors used it as a title—and it evolved into the words "Kaiser" and "Tsar."

❖ **Fact:** He crossed the Rubicon River. **Why?** In 49 BCE, by crossing this river with his army, Caesar defied the Senate and started a civil war. "Crossing the Rubicon" now means passing a point of no return.

❖ **Fact:** He was part of the First Triumvirate. **Why?** He joined forces with Pompey and Crassus to control Roman politics—until rivalries tore the alliance apart.

❖ **Fact:** He was a powerful speaker. **Why?** Caesar could sway crowds and senators alike with his speeches, helping him gain support and rise to power.

❖ **Fact:** His face appeared on coins. **Why?** Caesar was the first living Roman to have his image on coins—a bold move that showed his influence and ambition.

❖ **Fact:** His legacy still shapes the world. **Why?** Caesar's military, political, and cultural impact lasted far beyond his time, influencing how governments, languages, and leadership work even today.

Florence Nightingale

Born: 1820 – **Died:** 1910
Country: United Kingdom
Known for: Founder of modern nursing, medical reformer, and statistician
Fun Fact: She wrote over 150 books, reports, and papers in her lifetime!

Florence Nightingale wasn't afraid to challenge the rules of her time. With a lamp in her hand and science in her mind, she revolutionized nursing, saved lives through hygiene, and proved that data could be a powerful tool for change.

Fascinating Facts & Why They Matter

❖ **Fact:** She was known as "The Lady with the Lamp." **Why?** During the Crimean War, Florence walked through hospital wards at night with a lamp, comforting and caring for wounded soldiers.

❖ **Fact:** She was a pioneer in nursing. **Why?** In 1860, she founded the Nightingale School of Nursing in London—the first school to train nurses using scientific methods.

❖ **Fact:** She improved hospital sanitation. **Why?** Florence introduced strict hygiene rules that drastically lowered death rates in military hospitals.

❖ **Fact:** She was a statistician. **Why?** She used colorful charts and graphs to show how poor sanitation caused deaths, helping convince others to improve healthcare conditions.

❖ **Fact:** She wrote a famous book on nursing. **Why?** *Notes on Nursing* (1859) became a key textbook for nurses and helped shape how nursing is taught even today.

❖ **Fact:** She was awarded the Royal Red Cross. **Why?** Queen Victoria gave her this honor in 1883 to recognize her service to soldiers during the war.

❖ **Fact:** Her birthday is International Nurses Day. **Why?** May 12 is celebrated worldwide to honor nurses and their vital role in healthcare, thanks to Florence's legacy.

❖ **Fact:** She opened doors for women in medicine. **Why?** At a time when women were discouraged from studying medicine, Florence's work showed that women could lead in healthcare.

❖ **Fact:** She influenced hospital design. **Why?** Her ideas about fresh air, cleanliness, and proper lighting helped hospitals become safer and more effective places for healing.

❖ **Fact:** She kept learning throughout her life. **Why?** Even when ill and often bedridden, Florence kept writing and studying public health and statistics.

❖ **Fact:** Her family opposed her career. **Why?** In the 1800s, nursing wasn't seen as a proper job for women from wealthy families—but Florence followed her calling anyway.

- ❖ **Fact:** She received the Order of Merit. **Why?** In 1907, she became the first woman to receive this British honor for her extraordinary service to the nation.

- ❖ **Fact:** Her legacy lives on in nursing today. **Why?** Her focus on hygiene, compassion, and patient-centered care remains at the heart of modern nursing around the world.

Abraham Lincoln

Born: 1809 – **Died:** 1865
Country: United States
Known for: 16th President of the United States, ended slavery, led the country through the Civil War
Fun Fact: He was the tallest U.S. president—6 feet 4 inches!

Abraham Lincoln rose from a log cabin to the White House. With wisdom, honesty, and quiet strength, he led a divided nation through its greatest crisis and helped bring freedom to millions.

Fascinating Facts & Why They Matter

- **Fact:** He was the tallest U.S. president. **Why?** At 6 feet 4 inches (about 1.93 m), Lincoln's height made him stand out—literally! He often wore a tall stovepipe hat, making him look even taller.

- **Fact:** He was a self-taught lawyer. **Why?** Lincoln didn't go to law school. He read legal books on his own and passed the bar exam, showing that determination can open doors.

- **Fact:** He loved animals. **Why?** Lincoln had many pets, including a dog named Fido and a cat named Tabby. He even spared a turkey meant for Christmas dinner!

- **Fact:** He was a skilled wrestler. **Why?** As a young man, Lincoln won nearly 300 wrestling matches and lost only once. He's even in the National Wrestling Hall of Fame!

- **Fact:** His hat was more than just fashion. **Why?** He often stored important papers inside his tall hat while traveling. It was like a mobile briefcase!

❖ **Fact:** He was the first U.S. president with a beard. **Why?** After an 11-year-old girl named Grace Bedell wrote him a letter suggesting it would make him look more presidential, he grew one—and kept it.

❖ **Fact:** He made Thanksgiving a national holiday. **Why?** In 1863, Lincoln declared a national day of "Thanksgiving and Praise," helping shape the holiday as we know it today.

❖ **Fact:** His Gettysburg Address was only 272 words long. **Why?** In just a few short paragraphs, he honored fallen soldiers and reminded Americans why freedom and equality matter.

❖ **Fact:** He was the first U.S. president to be assassinated. **Why?** Lincoln was shot by John Wilkes Booth in 1865, just days after the Civil War ended. His death shocked the nation.

❖ **Fact:** His face is on the penny and the $5 bill. **Why?** These honors remind Americans of Lincoln's legacy as a leader who stood for unity and equality.

❖ **Fact:** He signed the Emancipation Proclamation. **Why?** This 1863 order freed enslaved people in Confederate states and marked a turning point in the fight against slavery.

❖ **Fact:** He had a patent for an invention. **Why?** Lincoln designed a device to lift boats over shallow water. He's the only U.S. president to ever hold a patent!

❖ **Fact:** His nickname was "Honest Abe." **Why?** People admired his fairness and honesty. He earned this nickname long before he became president.

❖ **Fact:** He grew up in a log cabin. **Why?** Born in rural Kentucky, Lincoln's humble beginnings showed that anyone—no matter how poor—could achieve great things.

❖ **Fact:** His favorite food was apples. **Why?** He loved eating them fresh and often kept one in his pocket for a snack.

Nikola Tesla

Born: 1856 – **Died:** 1943

Country: Born in the Austrian Empire (now Croatia), later moved to the United States

Known for: Inventor of alternating current (AC), the Tesla coil, and pioneer of wireless technology

Fun Fact: He was born during a lightning storm—and later worked with electricity!

Nikola Tesla was a scientist with lightning in his mind. His inventions helped power the modern world, and his imagination stretched far beyond his time—from wireless energy to predicting smartphones.

Fascinating Facts & Why They Matter

❖ **Fact:** He was born during a lightning storm. **Why?** Tesla arrived at midnight on July 10, 1856, during a powerful storm. Some said it was a sign he'd be connected to electricity—and they were right!

❖ **Fact:** He invented the Tesla coil. **Why?** Created in 1891, this device can generate high-voltage electricity. It's still used in some radios and can make lightning-like sparks!

❖ **Fact:** He had a photographic memory. **Why?** Tesla could memorize books and visualize machines entirely in his mind—he didn't even need to draw his inventions before building them.

❖ **Fact:** He spoke eight languages. **Why?** Tesla was fluent in Serbo-Croatian, English, German, French, Italian, Czech, Hungarian, and Latin. This helped him study and work around the world.

❖ **Fact:** He worked for Thomas Edison. **Why?** After moving to the U.S. in 1884, Tesla worked briefly for Edison, helping improve electrical devices—before their famous rivalry over AC vs. DC power began.

❖ **Fact:** He invented the alternating current (AC) system. **Why?** Tesla's AC system was more efficient than Edison's direct current (DC) and became the standard for distributing electricity around the world.

❖ **Fact:** He lit up the 1893 World's Fair. **Why?** Tesla wowed crowds by powering the entire Chicago fair with AC electricity, proving its safety and power.

❖ **Fact:** He held over 300 patents. **Why?** Tesla invented everything from motors to wireless technology. His ideas continue to shape our lives today.

❖ **Fact:** He dreamed of wireless electricity. **Why?** Tesla believed power could be sent through the air. He built the *Wardenclyffe Tower* to test this, but the project was never finished.

❖ **Fact:** He loved pigeons. **Why?** In his later years, Tesla cared for pigeons in New York. He said he had a deep connection with them, especially one he called his "special bird."

❖ **Fact:** A unit of measurement is named after him. **Why?** The *tesla* is a unit of magnetic field strength, honoring his groundbreaking work in electromagnetism.

❖ **Fact:** He predicted smartphones. **Why?** In 1926, Tesla described a future where people would carry a small device to communicate across the globe—just like today's phones.

❖ **Fact:** His inventions inspired modern technology. **Why?** From wireless communication to remote control, Tesla's work laid the foundation for many of today's devices.

❖ **Fact:** He's called "The Man Who Invented the 20th Century." **Why?** His ideas powered the world into the modern age—and beyond.

❖ **Fact:** Tesla's legacy lives on in electric cars. **Why?** The electric car company *Tesla*, founded by Elon Musk, was named in his honor to celebrate his vision and innovation.

Sacagawea

Born: 1788 – **Died:** 1812
Country: United States (Shoshone Nation)
Known for: Interpreter and guide for the Lewis and Clark expedition
Fun Fact: She carried her baby the entire journey—over 4,000 miles!

Sacagawea was just a teenager when she helped explore the American West. With a baby on her back and deep knowledge of nature and culture, she became a key part of one of the most important journeys in U.S. history.

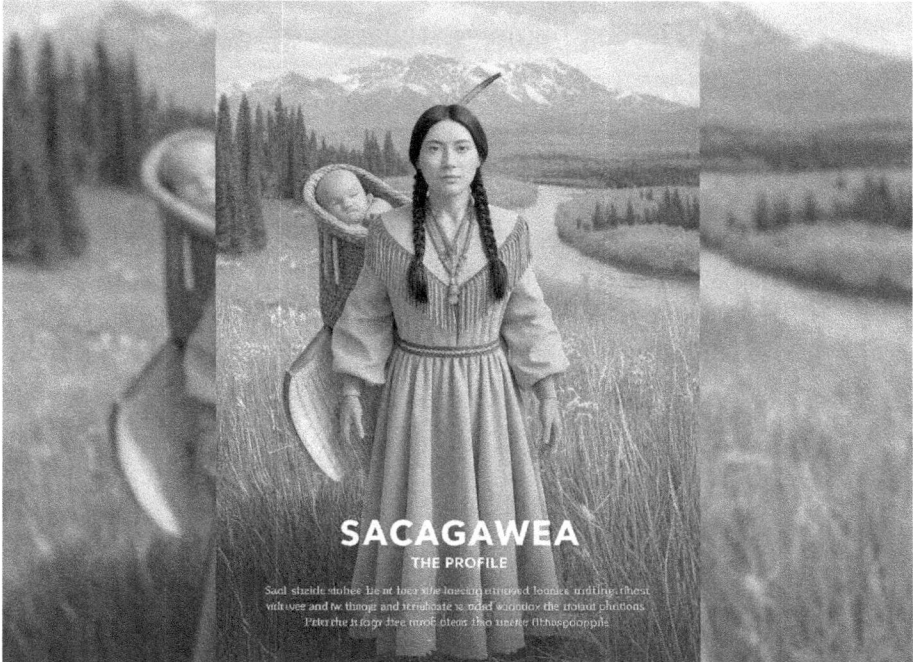

SACAGAWEA
THE PROFILE

Fascinating Facts & Why They Matter

❖ **Fact:** She was a teenage mom on an epic journey. **Why?** At about 16 years old, Sacagawea joined the Lewis and Clark expedition while carrying her infant son, Jean Baptiste. Her calm strength amazed the entire crew.

❖ **Fact:** She was a Shoshone interpreter. **Why?** Her ability to speak Shoshone and understand tribal customs helped the expedition communicate with Native American groups across the West.

❖ **Fact:** Her name means "Bird Woman." **Why?** In the Hidatsa language, "Sacagawea" translates to "Bird Woman," a name that reflects her heritage and identity.

❖ **Fact:** She helped find food for the expedition. **Why?** Using her knowledge of wild plants and herbs, Sacagawea gathered roots and berries—essential for feeding the group in tough conditions.

❖ **Fact:** Her presence helped ensure peace. **Why?** A young woman traveling with a baby signaled that the expedition was peaceful. War parties never traveled with women and children.

- ❖ **Fact:** She guided the group through the Rocky Mountains. **Why?** Her memory of the land and familiarity with mountain paths helped the explorers survive dangerous terrain.

- ❖ **Fact:** She is honored on a U.S. coin. **Why?** The *Sacagawea dollar*, first issued in 2000, recognizes her vital role in American history.

- ❖ **Fact:** She saved important supplies from a capsized boat. **Why?** When a boat tipped over, Sacagawea quickly rescued floating papers, maps, and journals—saving valuable information.

- ❖ **Fact:** She was reunited with her brother during the journey. **Why?** In a surprising moment, Sacagawea met her long-lost brother, Chief Cameahwait, whose help provided horses for the expedition.

- ❖ **Fact:** She traveled more than 4,000 miles. **Why?** From North Dakota to the Pacific Ocean and back, she journeyed across rivers, mountains, and plains—an extraordinary feat of endurance.

Winston Churchill

Born: 1874 – **Died:** 1965
Country: United Kingdom
Known for: British Prime Minister during World War II, Nobel Prize-winning writer, and famous orator
Fun Fact: He painted, laid bricks, and once escaped from prison — all before becoming Prime Minister!

Winston Churchill led Britain through its darkest hours with powerful words and unwavering determination. He was more than a leader—he was a storyteller, builder, artist, and true character in every sense.

- **Fact:** He was a talented painter.
  Why? Churchill created over 500 paintings, using art as a way to relax and find peace during stressful times.

- **Fact:** He won the Nobel Prize in Literature.
  Why? In 1953, he received the award for his writings and speeches, including detailed books on World War II.

- **Fact:** He had a pet parrot named Charlie.
  Why? Charlie was known for mimicking Churchill's voice and reportedly lived to be over 100 years old!

- **Fact:** He became an honorary American citizen.
  Why? In 1963, President Kennedy gave him this title for his leadership and friendship with the U.S. during WWII.

- **Fact:** He was a bricklayer.
  Why? Churchill loved building things by hand and even joined the Bricklayers Union for fun.

❖ **Fact:** He served as Prime Minister twice. **Why?** He led Britain during World War II (1940–1945) and returned to the role from 1951 to 1955.

❖ **Fact:** He had a speech impediment. **Why?** Despite his lisp, he became one of history's greatest speakers, inspiring millions with his words.

❖ **Fact:** He loved cigars.
Why? His cigar became a trademark, and he even had an oxygen mask designed so he could smoke in flight!

❖ **Fact:** He was a prisoner of war. **Why?** During the Boer War in South Africa, he was captured but escaped—a daring act that made him famous.

❖ **Fact:** He was a prolific writer. **Why?** Churchill wrote over 40 books and hundreds of articles, sharing history, politics, and personal stories.

❖ **Fact:** He had a unique fashion sense. **Why?** He wore bow ties, top hats, and a special "siren suit"—a one-piece outfit for air raids.

❖ **Fact:** He was a skilled orator. **Why?** His speeches, like *"We shall fight on the beaches,"* are remembered as some of the most powerful ever delivered.

❖ **Fact:** He served in Parliament for over 60 years. **Why?** Churchill worked in many government roles before and after his time as Prime Minister.

❖ **Fact:** He was an animal lover. **Why?** Churchill kept cats, dogs, and even a black swan named Toby at his estate.

❖ **Fact:** His mother was American. **Why?** Born in Brooklyn, Jennie Jerome gave Churchill strong ties to the United States.

Frida Kahlo

Born: 1907 – **Died:** 1954
Country: Mexico
Known for: Painter of deeply personal and symbolic works
Fun Fact: She turned her pain into powerful paintings that are now admired all over the world.

Frida Kahlo was a bold and brilliant artist who used her brush to paint not just pictures, but her soul. Her life was full of challenges, but she never stopped creating, inspiring others with her strength and passion.

Fascinating Facts & Why They Matter

❖ **Fact:** She painted over 140 artworks. **Why?** Frida used painting as a way to explore her emotions and tell her life story, especially through powerful self-portraits.

❖ **Fact:** She survived a serious bus accident. **Why?** At age 18, a crash left her with lifelong injuries. During her recovery, she began painting—starting a lifelong artistic journey.

❖ **Fact:** Her house is now a museum. **Why?** *La Casa Azul* (The Blue House) in Mexico City is where she lived and worked, and it's now a museum honoring her life.

❖ **Fact:** She was married to another famous artist. **Why?** Frida married Diego Rivera, a well-known Mexican muralist. Their dramatic relationship influenced both of their works.

❖ **Fact:** Her art is full of symbolism. **Why?** Frida used bright colors and traditional Mexican symbols to share deep ideas about identity, pain, and culture.

- ❖ **Fact:** She was a fashion icon. **Why?** Frida wore traditional Mexican dresses, flower crowns, and bold jewelry, turning her personal style into an artistic statement.

- ❖ **Fact:** Her paintings are in museums worldwide. **Why?** Frida's bold, emotional art is celebrated around the globe for its honesty and creativity.

- ❖ **Fact:** She had a pet deer. **Why?** Frida loved animals and kept many pets, including monkeys, parrots, and a deer named Granizo—who even appeared in her artwork.

- ❖ **Fact:** Her work was influenced by her heritage. **Why?** Frida proudly embraced her Mexican roots, adding indigenous traditions, myths, and colors to her art.

- ❖ **Fact:** She was a teacher. **Why?** Frida taught art at the National School of Painting in Mexico City, mentoring young artists with her creativity and passion.

Genghis Khan

Born: 1162 – **Died:** 1227
Country/Empire: Mongol Empire
Known for: Founding the largest contiguous empire in history
Fun Fact: He united nomadic tribes and ruled an empire that stretched from the Pacific Ocean to Europe!

Genghis Khan was a fierce and brilliant leader who re-shaped the world map. He led warriors across mountains and deserts, but he also built systems that connected people, ideas, and cultures.

Fascinating Facts & Why They Matter

❖ **Fact:** He created one of the largest empires in history. **Why?** By uniting Mongol tribes, he expanded his empire over 12 million square miles—from China to Europe.

❖ **Fact:** He was born with the name Temüjin. **Why?** He later took the title "Genghis Khan," meaning *universal ruler*, to reflect his ambition and success.

❖ **Fact:** His empire had a vast communication system. **Why?** He built the *Yam*, a relay system with horses and messengers that sped up communication across enormous distances.

❖ **Fact:** He promoted religious tolerance. **Why?** Genghis believed that allowing people to practice their own faiths would reduce conflict and unify the empire.

❖ **Fact:** His army excelled at horseback archery. **Why?** Mongol warriors were expert riders and archers, trained from childhood, making them nearly unstoppable in battle.

❖ **Fact:** He introduced a script for the Mongolian language. **Why?** He wanted to strengthen unity and administration across the empire, so he created a written form of Mongolian.

❖ **Fact:** His empire followed a legal code called the *Yassa*. **Why?** The *Yassa* set rules for justice, military behavior, and daily life, helping maintain order.

❖ **Fact:** His descendants ruled for generations. **Why?** His family continued his legacy—his grandson Kublai Khan ruled China and founded the Yuan Dynasty.

❖ **Fact:** His burial site is a mystery. **Why?** Legend says his burial party kept the location secret forever—no one knows where the great conqueror lies.

❖ **Fact:** He boosted trade along the Silk Road. **Why?** By protecting merchants and routes, Genghis helped goods, cultures, and ideas flow between East and West.

Helen Keller

Born: 1880 – **Died:** 1968
Country: United States
Known for: Author, activist, and the first deaf-blind person to earn a college degree
Fun Fact: She learned to "listen" by feeling words spelled on her hand!

Helen Keller lost her sight and hearing as a baby—but that didn't stop her. With courage, curiosity, and the help of her devoted teacher Anne Sullivan, she opened up to the world and became a voice for millions.

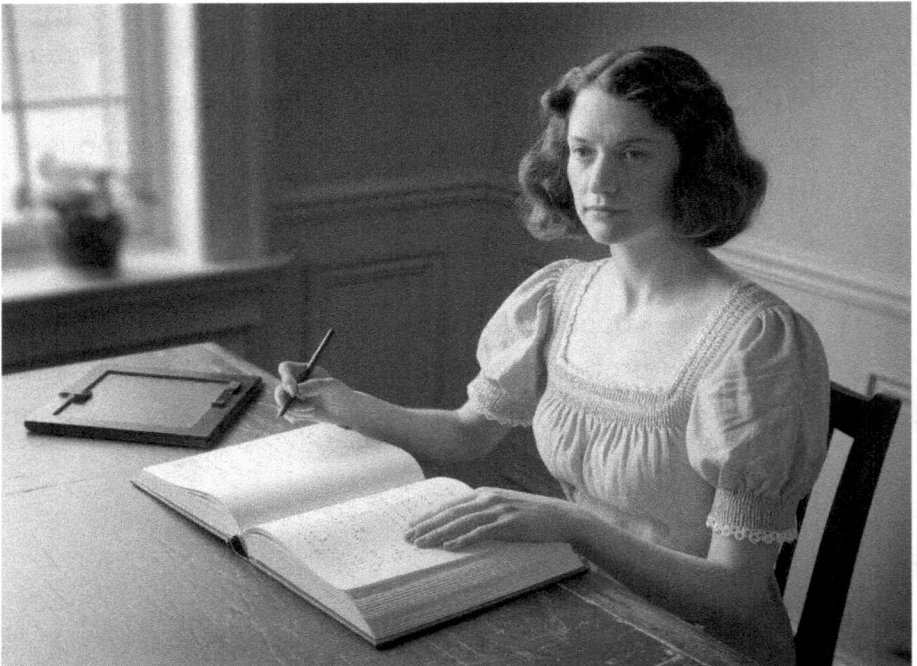

Fascinating Facts & Why They Matter

❖ **Fact:** She was the first deaf-blind person to earn a college degree.
Why? In 1904, she graduated from Radcliffe College, proving that disability does not limit intelligence or ambition.

❖ **Fact:** She learned to communicate using her sense of touch.
Why? Her teacher, Anne Sullivan, used fingerspelling into Helen's hand to teach her words, starting with "water."

❖ **Fact:** She wrote 12 published books.
Why? Her writings, especially *The Story of My Life*, inspired readers around the world and offered insight into her extraordinary journey.

❖ **Fact:** She was a world traveler.
Why? Helen visited 39 countries, advocating for people with disabilities and promoting education and inclusion.

❖ **Fact:** She was an advocate for people with disabilities.
Why? She worked to improve access to education and support, believing everyone deserves the chance to thrive.

❖ **Fact:** She met every U.S. president from Grover Cleveland to Lyndon B. Johnson.
Why? Her reputation as an influential activist brought her face-to-face with leaders who respected her work.

❖ **Fact:** She received the Presidential Medal of Freedom.
Why? In 1964, she was honored for her lifelong efforts to improve the lives of others.

❖ **Fact:** She co-founded the American Civil Liberties Union (ACLU).
Why? Helen believed in justice for all people, including those marginalized by society.

❖ **Fact:** She was a skilled public speaker.
Why? With the help of interpreters, she delivered speeches across the globe, inspiring countless audiences.

❖ **Fact:** Her life was the subject of a famous play and movie.
Why? *The Miracle Worker* tells how Helen and her teacher Anne broke through barriers—an unforgettable story of determination.

Nelson Mandela

Born: 1918 – **Died:** 2013
Country: South Africa
Known for: Anti-apartheid leader, political prisoner, and South Africa's first black president
Fun Fact: He was known for his bright "Madiba shirts" and warm, powerful smile.

Nelson Mandela fought for justice in South Africa and became a symbol of peace and forgiveness around the world. Even after spending 27 years in prison, he chose reconciliation over revenge.

Fascinating Facts & Why They Matter

❖ **Fact:** He was the first black president of South Africa. **Why?** In 1994, after apartheid ended, Mandela was elected in the country's first multiracial democratic election.

❖ **Fact:** He spent 27 years in prison. **Why?** He was jailed for fighting against apartheid and demanding equal rights for all South Africans.

❖ **Fact:** His prison number was 46664. **Why?** This number identified him on Robben Island, where he was imprisoned for 18 years of his sentence.

❖ **Fact:** He won the Nobel Peace Prize in 1993. **Why?** He was honored for his peaceful leadership in ending apartheid and building a democratic nation.

❖ **Fact:** His birth name was Rolihlahla. **Why?** In the Xhosa language, it means "pulling the branch of a tree" — or more playfully, "troublemaker."

❖ **Fact:** He studied law.
Why? He believed education was a powerful tool to fight injustice and became one of South Africa's first black lawyers.

❖ **Fact:** His autobiography is titled *Long Walk to Freedom*.
Why? It tells the inspiring story of his life, from rural child-hood to becoming a global symbol of peace.

❖ **Fact:** He was known for his colorful "Madiba shirts."
Why? Named after his clan, these shirts reflected his pride in his heritage and his personal style.

❖ **Fact:** He co-founded the African National Congress Youth League.
Why? He believed young people had the power to shape the future and led them in peaceful protest against apart-heid.

❖ **Fact:** Mandela Day is celebrated on July 18th.
Why? On his birthday, people around the world are en-couraged to spend 67 minutes doing something good — one minute for every year he spent serving his people.

Marco Polo

Born: 1254 – **Died:** 1324
Country: Italy (Republic of Venice)
Known for: Explorer and storyteller who traveled to Asia and wrote about his adventures
Fun Fact: His travels inspired the age of exploration and changed how Europeans saw the world!

Marco Polo was one of the first Europeans to explore the East and share detailed stories about the cultures, people, and marvels he encountered. His book opened the imagination of generations to the wonders of Asia.

📌 Fascinating Facts & Why They Matter

❖ **Fact:** Marco Polo traveled to China when he was just 17 years old.
Why? He set out with his father and uncle on a journey that took more than three years to complete across the Silk Road.

❖ **Fact:** His journey covered more than 15,000 miles.
Why? He traveled by both land and sea, visiting regions like Persia, India, and China—an extraordinary adventure for his time!

❖ **Fact:** Marco Polo served in the court of Kublai Khan.
Why? The Mongol emperor valued Marco's intelligence and made him a special envoy, sending him on important missions.

❖ **Fact:** He introduced Europe to paper money.
Why? Marco described how the Chinese used paper currency, which was an entirely new idea to Europeans.

❖ **Fact:** His book inspired Christopher Columbus.
Why? *The Travels of Marco Polo* described exotic lands

and wealth that sparked European exploration—including Columbus's voyage.

❖ **Fact:** He was captured and imprisoned. **Why?** During a war between Venice and Genoa, Marco was taken prisoner and dictated his adventures to a fellow inmate, Rustichello da Pisa.

❖ **Fact:** His book was originally called *The Description of the World*.
 Why? It fascinated readers with tales of distant places, unusual customs, and incredible riches.

❖ **Fact:** He described the wonders of the Silk Road. **Why?** This trade route connected East and West, and Marco's stories helped Europeans learn about it for the first time.

❖ **Fact:** He claimed to have seen unicorns. **Why?** He likely saw rhinoceroses but described them based on the legends of his time, showing how travel reshaped myths.

❖ **Fact:** His travels lasted 24 years. **Why?** He spent many years exploring, working, and learning in Asia before finally returning to Venice with tales no one could believe!

Mother Teresa

Born: 1910 – **Died:** 1997
Country: Born in Macedonia, lived and worked in India
Known for: Catholic nun and missionary who devoted her life to the poor
Fun Fact: She started her mission with only 5 rupees (less than a dollar)!

Mother Teresa spent her life caring for the sick, poor, and forgotten. Her small acts of kindness grew into a global mission that continues to help people in need today.

Fascinating Facts & Why They Matter

❖ **Fact:** Mother Teresa was born in Macedonia. **Why?** She was born on August 26, 1910, in Skopje, which is now the capital of North Macedonia.

❖ **Fact:** Her real name was Anjezë Gonxhe Bojaxhiu. **Why?** When she became a nun, she chose the name Teresa after Saint Thérèse of Lisieux, who inspired her with her simple acts of love.

❖ **Fact:** She founded the Missionaries of Charity. **Why?** In 1950, she started this group to serve "the poorest of the poor" in India and around the world.

❖ **Fact:** She won the Nobel Peace Prize in 1979. **Why?** Her selfless service to those suffering from poverty and illness earned her global recognition.

❖ **Fact:** She opened her first school in a slum. **Why?** She believed education could give hope and dignity to children living in poverty.

❖ **Fact:** She was canonized as a saint. **Why?** In 2016, the Catholic Church declared her a saint for her life of service and miracles attributed to her.

❖ **Fact:** Her work spread to over 130 countries. **Why?** The Missionaries of Charity grew into an international organization that continues her mission today.

❖ **Fact:** She received the Bharat Ratna. **Why?** India awarded her its highest civilian honor in 1980 for her humanitarian efforts.

❖ **Fact:** She started her mission with just 5 rupees. **Why?** With only a tiny sum and a big heart, she relied on faith and generosity to build schools, clinics, and homes.

❖ **Fact:** Her first home for the dying was called *Nirmal Hriday*. **Why?** It means "Pure Heart" in Hindi, and it gave dignity and care to those who were dying alone on the streets.

Isaac Newton

Born: 1642 – **Died:** 1727
Country: England
Known for: Discovering gravity, inventing calculus, and revolutionizing physics
Fun Fact: He was born on Christmas Day!

Sir Isaac Newton was a curious and quiet genius who observed the world with thoughtful eyes. His discoveries changed the way we understand the universe — from the fall of an apple to the motion of the planets.

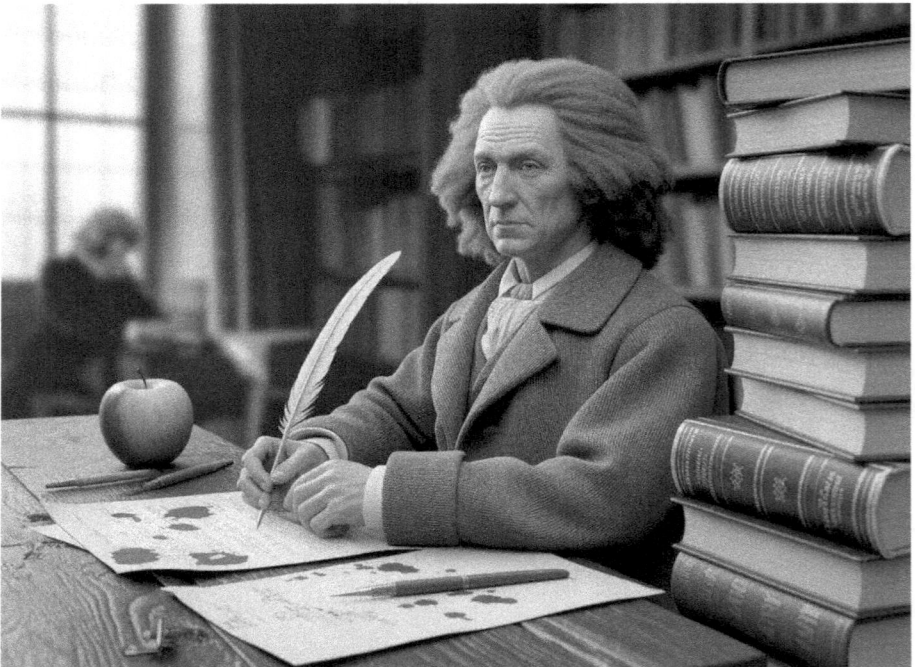

Fascinating Facts & Why They Matter

❖ **Fact:** Isaac Newton was born on Christmas Day.
Why? He was born on December 25, 1642, according to the Julian calendar used in England at the time.

❖ **Fact:** Newton discovered gravity by watching an apple fall.
Why? This simple observation is what sparked his thoughts about why objects fall to the ground — leading to his theory of gravity.

❖ **Fact:** Newton invented calculus.
Why? He needed a new kind of math to explain changing motion, like the orbits of planets — so he created one!

❖ **Fact:** Newton's laws of motion changed the world.
Why? His three laws explain how everything moves, from bouncing balls to rockets — and are still taught in science class today.

❖ **Fact:** Newton was a member of Parliament.
Why? He represented Cambridge University, although he is said to have spoken very little while in office.

❖ **Fact:** Newton was knighted by Queen Anne. **Why?** In 1705, he was honored for his work in science and became "Sir Isaac Newton."

❖ **Fact:** Newton built the first practical reflecting telescope. **Why?** By using mirrors instead of lenses, he improved image clarity — a design still used in modern telescopes.

❖ **Fact:** Newton wrote a book called *Principia Mathematica*. **Why?** This groundbreaking book explained gravity and motion, laying the foundation for classical physics.

❖ **Fact:** Newton was also an alchemist. **Why?** He spent years trying to turn metals into gold — something many scientists believed possible at the time.

❖ **Fact:** Newton had a pet dog named Diamond. **Why?** According to legend, the dog knocked over a candle and burned some of Newton's valuable papers.

❖ **Fact:** Newton was a professor at Cambridge University. **Why?** He was appointed Lucasian Professor of Mathematics, a role later held by Stephen Hawking.

❖ **Fact:** Newton studied the nature of light and color. **Why?** Using a prism, he discovered that white light contains all the colors of the rainbow.

❖ **Fact:** Newton was a very private person. **Why?** He worked alone and sometimes kept his discoveries secret for years before sharing them.

❖ **Fact:** Newton's face appeared on British banknotes. **Why?** From 1978 to 1988, his image was on the one-pound note as a tribute to his scientific achievements.

❖ **Fact:** Newton's work inspired future scientists. **Why?** His ideas shaped modern science and paved the way for thinkers like Albert Einstein.

Anne Frank

Born: 1929 – **Died:** 1945
Country: Born in Germany, lived in the Netherlands
Known for: Writing a diary while hiding during the Holocaust
Fun Fact: She gave her diary the name "Kitty," imagining it as a trusted friend.

Anne Frank was a young girl with a bright mind and a big heart. Her diary captured the thoughts, fears, and hopes of someone growing up in one of the darkest times in history. Her words still inspire millions today.

Fascinating Facts & Why They Matter

❖ **Fact:** Anne Frank wrote her famous diary while hiding from the Nazis.
Why? She and her family hid in a secret annex in Amsterdam for over two years during World War II.

❖ **Fact:** Anne Frank's diary was first published in 1947.
Why? Her father, Otto Frank, was the only family member to survive the Holocaust and decided to share her story with the world.

❖ **Fact:** Anne Frank's diary has been translated into over 70 languages.
Why? Her story of courage and hope has touched people all around the globe.

❖ **Fact:** Anne Frank was born in Germany.
Why? She was born on June 12, 1929, in Frankfurt, but her family moved to the Netherlands to escape Nazi persecution.

❖ **Fact:** Anne Frank named her diary "Kitty."
Why? She imagined her diary as a friend she could confide in during her time in hiding.

❖ **Fact:** The secret annex was hidden behind a bookcase. **Why?** The entrance to their hiding place was cleverly concealed to keep it a secret from the outside world.

❖ **Fact:** Anne Frank dreamed of becoming a writer. **Why?** She hoped to publish a book about her experiences after the war, which she began revising while in hiding.

❖ **Fact:** Anne Frank's family was discovered in 1944. **Why?** They were betrayed by an unknown informant and arrested by the Nazis.

❖ **Fact:** Anne Frank died in a concentration camp. **Why?** She and her sister Margot were sent to Bergen-Belsen, where they both died of typhus in early 1945.

❖ **Fact:** The Anne Frank House is now a museum. **Why?** The building where she hid has been preserved to educate visitors about her life and the Holocaust.

Benjamin Franklin

Born: 1706 – **Died:** 1790
Country: United States
Known for: Founding Father, inventor, writer, scientist
Fun Fact: He once flew a kite in a thunderstorm—to study electricity!

Benjamin Franklin was a man of many talents. From inventing everyday items to helping create a new nation, he used curiosity and determination to shape the world around him. His ideas still shine brightly today.

📌 Fascinating Facts & Why They Matter

❖ **Fact:** Benjamin Franklin was one of the Founding Fathers of the United States!
Why? He helped draft the Declaration of Independence in 1776, which announced America's freedom from British rule.

❖ **Fact:** Benjamin Franklin was a famous inventor!
Why? He created the lightning rod, bifocal glasses, and the Franklin stove, which improved heating efficiency.

❖ **Fact:** Benjamin Franklin conducted experiments with electricity!
Why? He flew a kite during a thunderstorm to prove that lightning is a form of electricity.

❖ **Fact:** Benjamin Franklin started the first public library in America!
Why? He founded the Library Company of Philadelphia in 1731 to share books with others.

❖ **Fact:** Benjamin Franklin was a skilled diplomat!
Why? He helped secure France's support during the American Revolution, which was crucial for victory.

❖ **Fact:** Benjamin Franklin was a prolific writer!
Why? He wrote *Poor Richard's Almanack*, a popular publication filled with witty sayings and advice.

❖ **Fact:** Benjamin Franklin was a self-taught scientist!
Why? He had little formal education but taught himself through reading and experimentation.

❖ **Fact:** Benjamin Franklin was the first Postmaster General of the United States!
Why? He organized the postal system to improve communication across the colonies.

❖ **Fact:** Benjamin Franklin loved music and played several instruments!
Why? He played the violin, harp, and guitar, and even invented a musical instrument called the glass armonica.

❖ **Fact:** Benjamin Franklin was an advocate for education!
Why? He helped establish the University of Pennsylvania, one of the first universities in America.

❖ **Fact:** Benjamin Franklin was a strong supporter of the abolition of slavery!
Why? He became president of the Pennsylvania Society for Promoting the Abolition of Slavery in 1787.

❖ **Fact:** Benjamin Franklin's face is on the $100 bill!
Why? He is honored for his contributions to American history and his role as a statesman and inventor.

❖ **Fact:** Benjamin Franklin was a master of self-improvement!
Why? He created a list of 13 virtues to live by, such as temperance and humility, to better himself.

❖ **Fact:** Benjamin Franklin was a talented swimmer!
Why? He swam across the Thames River in London and even invented swim fins to improve his speed.

❖ **Fact:** Benjamin Franklin was a member of the American Philosophical Society!
Why? He founded this organization to promote knowledge and scientific discovery.

Catherine the Great

Born: 1729 – **Died:** 1796
Country: Russia (born in Prussia)
Known for: Empress of Russia, reformer, arts patron
Fun Fact: She exchanged letters with famous philosophers like Voltaire!

Catherine the Great was one of the most powerful women in history. Though she was born outside of Russia, she rose to lead the empire for over three decades. With intelligence and ambition, she expanded Russia's borders and championed education, art, and modern ideas.

Fascinating Facts & Why They Matter

❖ **Fact:** Catherine the Great was the longest-ruling female leader of Russia!
Why? She reigned for 34 years, from 1762 to 1796, bringing significant changes to the country.

❖ **Fact:** Catherine the Great was not originally from Russia!
Why? She was born in Prussia, which is now part of Poland, and her birth name was Sophie Friederike Auguste von Anhalt-Zerbst-Dornburg.

❖ **Fact:** Catherine the Great expanded the Russian Empire!
Why? She added over 200,000 square miles to Russia's territory, including parts of Poland, Ukraine, and Crimea.

❖ **Fact:** Catherine the Great was a patron of the arts!
Why? She founded the Hermitage Museum in St. Petersburg, which is one of the largest and oldest museums in the world.

❖ **Fact:** Catherine the Great corresponded with famous philosophers!
Why? She exchanged letters with Enlightenment thinkers

like Voltaire and Diderot, discussing ideas about government and society.

❖ **Fact:** Catherine the Great improved education in Russia! **Why?** She established the Smolny Institute, the first state-funded school for girls in Russia, and promoted education reforms.

❖ **Fact:** Catherine the Great was known for her intelligence and wit!
Why? She was fluent in several languages, including Russian, German, and French, and was known for her sharp mind.

❖ **Fact:** Catherine the Great modernized Russia's legal system!
Why? She introduced the "Nakaz," a document that aimed to reform the legal code and promote equality and justice.

❖ **Fact:** Catherine the Great loved gardening!
Why? She created beautiful gardens at her palaces, including the famous Tsarskoye Selo, which is now a UNESCO World Heritage site.

❖ **Fact:** Catherine the Great was a prolific writer!
Why? She wrote plays, memoirs, and even a guide to education, showcasing her diverse interests and talents.

Galileo Galilei

Born: 1564 – **Died:** 1642
Country: Italy
Known for: Astronomer, physicist, inventor
Fun Fact: He improved the telescope and discovered moons around Jupiter!

Galileo Galilei was a brilliant scientist who changed how we see the universe. With his telescope, he explored the stars, challenged old beliefs, and helped lay the foundation for modern science. Even when his ideas caused controversy, Galileo never stopped searching for the truth.

Fascinating Facts & Why They Matter

❖ **Fact:** Galileo Galilei was the first to use a telescope to study the stars!
  Why? In 1609, he built his own telescope and discovered moons orbiting Jupiter, proving not everything revolves around Earth.

❖ **Fact:** Galileo discovered that the Milky Way is made up of countless stars!
  Why? By pointing his telescope at the Milky Way, he saw it was not just a cloud but a collection of stars.

❖ **Fact:** Galileo's observations supported the idea that the Earth orbits the Sun!
  Why? He saw phases of Venus similar to the Moon's, which only made sense if Venus orbited the Sun.

❖ **Fact:** Galileo discovered sunspots on the Sun!
  Why? He noticed dark spots moving across the Sun's surface, showing that the Sun rotates.

❖ **Fact:** Galileo was put on trial for his scientific beliefs!
  Why? His support for the Sun-centered solar system

challenged the Church's teachings, leading to house arrest.

* ❖ **Fact:** Galileo improved the design of the telescope! **Why?** He made lenses that magnified objects up to 20 times, allowing him to see further into space.

* ❖ **Fact:** Galileo discovered the four largest moons of Jupiter! **Why?** He named them Io, Europa, Ganymede, and Callisto, and they are now known as the Galilean moons.

* ❖ **Fact:** Galileo was a skilled mathematician! **Why?** He used math to explain the laws of motion and the behavior of falling objects.

* ❖ **Fact:** Galileo's work laid the foundation for modern physics! **Why?** His studies on motion and gravity influenced later scientists like Isaac Newton.

* ❖ **Fact:** Galileo was a professor at the University of Pisa! **Why?** He taught mathematics and conducted experiments that challenged traditional beliefs.

❖ **Fact:** Galileo wrote a book called "The Starry Messenger"! **Why?** Published in 1610, it shared his astronomical discoveries with the world.

❖ **Fact:** Galileo discovered that objects fall at the same rate regardless of their weight!
Why? He famously dropped two spheres of different weights from the Leaning Tower of Pisa to prove it.

❖ **Fact:** Galileo's father was a musician!
Why? Vincenzo Galilei was a composer and music theorist, influencing Galileo's interest in the arts and sciences.

❖ **Fact**: Galileo was born in Pisa, Italy, in 1564!
Why? His birthplace is famous for its leaning tower, and he later moved to Florence for his studies.

❖ **Fact:** Galileo's work was banned by the Catholic Church!
Why? His writings were placed on the Church's Index of Forbidden Books until 1835.

Harriet Beecher Stowe

Born: 1811 – **Died:** 1896
Country: United States
Known for: Author, abolitionist
Fun Fact: Her book *Uncle Tom's Cabin* sold 300,000 copies in just one year!

Harriet Beecher Stowe was a powerful writer who used her words to fight against slavery. Her most famous book helped open people's eyes to injustice and inspired many to take action. She believed that stories could change the world—and hers did.

Fascinating Facts & Why They Matter

❖ **Fact:** Harriet Beecher Stowe wrote *Uncle Tom's Cabin*, a famous anti-slavery novel!
Why? Published in 1852, it sold 300,000 copies in its first year and helped change public opinion about slavery.

❖ **Fact:** Harriet Beecher Stowe was inspired by the stories of escaped slaves!
Why? She met people who had fled slavery and used their experiences to create realistic characters in her book.

❖ **Fact:** Harriet Beecher Stowe's book was banned in the South!
Why? *Uncle Tom's Cabin* was seen as a threat to the pro-slavery society, leading to its ban in many Southern states.

❖ **Fact:** Harriet Beecher Stowe met President Abraham Lincoln!
Why? In 1862, Lincoln reportedly greeted her by saying, "So you're the little woman who wrote the book that started this great war."

- ❖ **Fact:** Harriet Beecher Stowe was a teacher before becoming a writer!
  Why? She taught at the Hartford Female Seminary, a school founded by her sister, where she educated young women.

- ❖ **Fact:** Harriet Beecher Stowe wrote more than 30 books!
  Why? Besides *Uncle Tom's Cabin*, she wrote novels, travel books, and collections of articles and essays.

- ❖ **Fact:** Harriet Beecher Stowe was part of a famous family!
  Why? Her father, Lyman Beecher, was a well-known preacher, and her brother, Henry Ward Beecher, was a famous abolitionist.

- ❖ **Fact:** Harriet Beecher Stowe's book was turned into a play!
  Why? *Uncle Tom's Cabin* was adapted for the stage, spreading its message even further across the country.

- ❖ **Fact:** Harriet Beecher Stowe moved to Florida later in life!
  Why? She and her husband bought a home in Mandarin, Florida, where she continued to write and advocate for social causes.

- ❖ **Fact:** Harriet Beecher Stowe's work influenced the abolitionist movement!

Why? Her vivid portrayal of the harsh realities of slavery inspired many to join the fight against it.

Ludwig van Beethoven

Born: 1770 – **Died:** 1827
Country: Germany (later Austria)
Known for: Legendary composer and pianist
Fun Fact: He kept composing even after he went completely deaf!

Ludwig van Beethoven was a musical genius whose powerful and emotional compositions helped shape the future of classical music. Even when he could no longer hear, his creativity never stopped!

Fascinating Facts & Why They Matter

❖ **Fact:** Beethoven began losing his hearing in his late 20s. **Why?** Despite going deaf, he kept composing master-pieces, using the vibrations of the piano to "feel" the music.

❖ **Fact:** Beethoven wrote nine symphonies. **Why?** These works are some of the most famous in classical music—especially the Ninth, which includes the beloved "Ode to Joy."

❖ **Fact:** Beethoven was born in Bonn, Germany, in 1770. **Why?** His birthplace is now a museum where visitors can learn about his extraordinary life.

❖ **Fact:** Beethoven's father wanted him to be a child prodigy like Mozart. **Why?** He pushed young Ludwig to practice hard, hoping he would become a musical superstar.

❖ **Fact:** Beethoven composed *Für Elise*. **Why?** This charming piano piece is still one of the first classical songs many students learn to play.

❖ **Fact:** Beethoven helped move music from the Classical to the Romantic era.
Why? His music added deep emotion and drama, inspiring generations of composers.

❖ **Fact:** *Moonlight Sonata* is one of Beethoven's most famous works.
Why? Its haunting melody has captivated listeners for over 200 years.

❖ **Fact:** Beethoven had a fiery temper.
Why? He was passionate about his music and had high standards, which sometimes led to disagreements.

❖ **Fact:** His *Fifth Symphony* is famous for its first four notes.
Why? The "da-da-da-DUM" is one of the most recognizable motifs in music history.

❖ **Fact:** Beethoven faced many health problems.
Why? Despite illness and deafness, he never gave up on creating music.

❖ **Fact:** The *Eroica Symphony* was originally dedicated to Napoleon.
Why? Beethoven admired Napoleon's ideals but with-

drew the dedication when Napoleon crowned himself emperor.

❖ **Fact:** His music was played at the fall of the Berlin Wall in 1989.
Why? *Ode to Joy* became a symbol of hope, freedom, and unity.

❖ **Fact:** Beethoven died in Vienna in 1827.
Why? His funeral drew thousands, proving how beloved he had become.

❖ **Fact:** *Pastoral Symphony* was inspired by nature.
Why? Beethoven loved long walks in the countryside, which inspired this joyful, earthy music.

❖ **Fact:** Beethoven still inspires musicians today.
Why? His passion, creativity, and courage in the face of deafness make him one of history's most inspiring artists.

Sitting Bull

Born: circa 1831 – **Died:** 1890
Country/Region: United States (Lakota Sioux Nation)
Known for: Native American leader and symbol of resistance
Fun Fact: He once toured the U.S. with Buffalo Bill's Wild West Show!

● Sitting Bull was a brave and wise Lakota Sioux chief who stood up for his people's land, rights, and traditions. He is remembered for his leadership, courage, and powerful spirit.

Fascinating Facts & Why They Matter

❖ **Fact:** Sitting Bull was a famous leader of the Lakota Sioux tribe.
Why? He was known for his bravery and strong leadership during resistance against U.S. government policies.

❖ **Fact:** Sitting Bull played a key role in the Battle of Little Bighorn.
Why? In 1876, he led his people to victory against General Custer's army—a major moment in Native American history.

❖ **Fact:** Sitting Bull had a vision of victory before the Battle of Little Bighorn.
Why? He saw soldiers falling into his camp, inspiring confidence and unity among his warriors.

❖ **Fact:** Sitting Bull was a skilled diplomat.
Why? He worked to bring together different Native tribes to resist U.S. expansion into their lands.

❖ **Fact:** Sitting Bull toured with Buffalo Bill's Wild West Show.

Why? He shared Native culture with the public and earned money to support his people.

- ❖ **Fact:** Sitting Bull was a spiritual leader.
  Why? As a respected medicine man, he performed sacred ceremonies and offered spiritual guidance.

- ❖ **Fact:** Sitting Bull was born in present-day South Dakota.
  Why? He was born near the Grand River, in an area that later became part of the United States.

- ❖ **Fact:** Sitting Bull was arrested by the U.S. government.
  Why? After years of resistance, he surrendered in 1881 and was held as a prisoner for two years.

- ❖ **Fact:** Sitting Bull's name means "Buffalo Bull Who Sits Down."
  Why? His name symbolized strength, calm power, and standing firm like a buffalo facing danger.

- ❖ **Fact:** Sitting Bull was killed in 1890.
  Why? Authorities feared he would join the Ghost Dance movement, and he was shot during an attempted arrest.

❖ **Fact:** Sitting Bull's legacy lives on. **Why?** He is honored as a symbol of Native American resistance and a defender of his people's rights and traditions.

Vincent van Gogh

Born: 1853 – **Died:** 1890

Country/Region: The Netherlands

Known for: Post-Impressionist painter

Fun Fact: He painted some of his most famous works while living in a mental asylum!

🎨 Vincent van Gogh was a brilliant and emotional artist whose bold brushstrokes and colorful paintings changed the art world forever. Though unappreciated in his lifetime, he is now considered one of the greatest painters in history.

Fascinating Facts & Why They Matter

❖ **Fact:** Vincent van Gogh painted over 900 paintings in just 10 years.
Why? He was incredibly productive, creating master-pieces like *Starry Night* and *Sunflowers* in a short period.

❖ **Fact:** Van Gogh only sold one painting during his lifetime.
Why? Despite his talent, he struggled to gain recognition and lived in poverty.

❖ **Fact:** Van Gogh cut off part of his own ear.
Why? After a heated argument with fellow artist Paul Gauguin, he famously injured himself in a moment of distress.

❖ **Fact:** Van Gogh was born in the Netherlands in 1853.
Why? He grew up in a small village called Zundert, where his love for nature began.

❖ **Fact:** Van Gogh's *Starry Night* was painted while he was in a mental asylum.
Why? He found inspiration in the view from his window, creating one of his most iconic works.

❖ **Fact:** Van Gogh's brother, Theo, was his biggest supporter.
Why? Theo provided financial and emotional support, encouraging Vincent's artistic journey.

❖ **Fact:** Van Gogh used bold colors and expressive brushstrokes.
Why? His unique style set him apart from other artists and influenced future movements like Expressionism.

❖ **Fact:** Van Gogh's paintings are now worth millions.
Why? Although he was not appreciated in his time, his work is now celebrated worldwide.

❖ **Fact:** Van Gogh was inspired by Japanese art.
Why? He admired the simplicity and beauty of Japanese prints, which influenced his compositions and use of color.

❖ **Fact:** Van Gogh's *The Bedroom* depicts his own room in Arles, France.
Why? He painted it to show his peaceful personal space using vibrant and symbolic colors.

❖ **Fact:** Van Gogh struggled with mental health issues.
Why? Despite these challenges, he continued to create deeply emotional and expressive art.

❖ **Fact:** Van Gogh's *Irises* was painted during his stay at a mental hospital.
Why? He found comfort in painting the flowers and gardens around him.

❖ **Fact:** Van Gogh's work was influenced by Impressionism.
Why? He admired the use of light and color, which he incorporated into his expressive style.

❖ **Fact:** Van Gogh's *The Starry Night* is one of the most recognized paintings in the world.
Why? Its swirling skies and vibrant palette continue to captivate viewers and inspire artists.

❖ **Fact:** Van Gogh's legacy lives on through his art.
Why? His powerful creativity and emotional depth have made him one of the most beloved artists in history.

Susan B. Anthony

Born: 1820 – **Died:** 1906
Country/Region: United States
Known for: Women's rights activist and suffragist
Fun Fact: She was the first woman to appear on a circulating U.S. coin!

📷 Susan B. Anthony was a fearless leader in the fight for women's rights in America. Her powerful voice and tireless activism helped spark a movement that would one day lead to women gaining the right to vote.

Fascinating Facts & Why They Matter

❖ **Fact:** Susan B. Anthony was a key leader in the women's suffrage movement.
Why? She fought tirelessly for women's right to vote, helping to pave the way for the 19th Amendment.

❖ **Fact:** Susan B. Anthony was born in 1820.
Why? She was born in Adams, Massachusetts, and grew up in a Quaker family that valued social justice.

❖ **Fact:** Susan B. Anthony was arrested for voting.
Why? In 1872, she voted illegally in the presidential election to challenge laws that barred women from voting.

❖ **Fact:** Susan B. Anthony co-founded the National Woman Suffrage Association.
Why? She and Elizabeth Cady Stanton started the organization in 1869 to fight for women's voting rights.

❖ **Fact:** Susan B. Anthony appeared on U.S. currency.
Why? She was the first woman to be featured on a circulating U.S. coin, the Susan B. Anthony dollar, in 1979.

❖ **Fact:** Susan B. Anthony was a teacher before becoming an   activist.

Why? She taught at a Quaker school, where she saw firsthand the inequalities faced by women and girls.

- ❖ **Fact:** Susan B. Anthony gave over 75 speeches a year.
  Why? She traveled across the country to advocate for women's rights and inspire others to join the cause.

- ❖ **Fact:** Susan B. Anthony never married.
  Why? She believed that marriage would limit her independence and ability to fight for women's rights.

- ❖ **Fact:** Susan B. Anthony's work led to the 19th Amendment.
  Why? Although she didn't live to see it, her efforts were crucial in securing women's right to vote in 1920.

- ❖ **Fact:** Susan B. Anthony was friends with Frederick Douglass.
  Why? They both worked for social reform and supported each other's efforts for equality.

- ❖ **Fact:** Susan B. Anthony's childhood home is a museum.
  Why? The Susan B. Anthony Birthplace Museum in Massachusetts honors her legacy and educates visitors about her life.

❖ **Fact:** Susan B. Anthony was a skilled organizer. **Why?** She helped organize the first women's rights convention in Seneca Falls, New York, in 1848.

❖ **Fact:** Susan B. Anthony's motto was "Failure is impossible."
Why? She believed in perseverance and never giving up on the fight for equality.

❖ **Fact:** Susan B. Anthony was honored with a U.S. postage stamp.
Why? In 1936, the U.S. Postal Service issued a stamp to commemorate her contributions to women's rights.

❖ **Fact:** Susan B. Anthony's legacy continues to inspire. **Why?** Her dedication to equality and justice motivates new generations to advocate for their rights.

Confucius

Born: 551 B.C. – **Died:** 479 B.C.
Country/Region: Ancient China
Known for: Philosopher, teacher, and founder of Confucianism
Fun Fact: His birthday is celebrated as Teacher's Day in China!

📚 **Confucius was a wise teacher and philosopher whose ideas shaped Chinese society for thousands of years. He believed in kindness, respect, and learning, and his sayings are still shared around the world today.**

Fascinating Facts & Why They Matter

❖ **Fact:** Confucius was born over 2,500 years ago! **Why?** He was born in 551 B.C. in the state of Lu, which is now part of modern-day China.

❖ **Fact:** Confucius was a teacher and philosopher! **Why?** He taught about ethics, good behavior, and the importance of family and respect.

❖ **Fact:** Confucius believed in the "Golden Rule"! **Why?** He taught that you should treat others the way you want to be treated.

❖ **Fact:** Confucius wrote many famous sayings! **Why?** His wise words were collected in a book called *The Analects*, which is still read today.

❖ **Fact:** Confucius valued education highly! **Why?** He believed that learning and knowledge were key to becoming a better person.

- ❖ **Fact:** Confucius had many students! **Why?** His teachings attracted followers who spread his ideas throughout China.
- ❖ **Fact:** Confucius' ideas influenced Chinese culture! **Why?** His teachings became the foundation for Chinese society and government for centuries.

- ❖ **Fact:** Confucius believed in leading by example! **Why?** He thought that rulers should be virtuous and set a good example for their people.

- ❖ **Fact:** Confucius' teachings focus on five key relationships! **Why?** He emphasized the importance of relationships between ruler and subject, parent and child, husband and wife, older and younger siblings, and friends.

- ❖ **Fact:** Confucius' ideas are still studied today! **Why?** His teachings on morality and ethics continue to inspire people around the world.

- ❖ **Fact:** Confucius' birthday is celebrated as Teacher's Day in China! **Why?** His contributions to education and philosophy are honored every year on September 28th.

❖ **Fact:** Confucius believed in the importance of rituals! **Why?** He thought that rituals helped maintain social order and respect within society.

❖ **Fact:** Confucius' family name was Kong! **Why?** His full name was Kong Qiu, and he is often referred to as Kong Fuzi, meaning "Master Kong."

❖ **Fact:** Confucius' teachings were not widely accepted during his lifetime!
Why? It was only after his death that his ideas gained popularity and became central to Chinese culture.

❖ **Fact:** Confucius' philosophy is known as Confucianism! **Why?** His teachings formed the basis of a system of thought that has influenced many aspects of life in East Asia.

Pablo Picasso

Born: 1881 – **Died:** 1973
Country/Region: Spain
Known for: Painter, sculptor, and founder of Cubism
Fun Fact: His first word was "pencil"!

🎨 Pablo Picasso was one of the most influential artists in history. Known for constantly reinventing his style, he painted, sculpted, drew, and even wrote plays. From his early masterpieces to his bold experiments, Picasso left behind a world of color and imagination that still inspires today.

Fascinating Facts & Why They Matter

❖ **Fact:** Pablo Picasso was a child prodigy! **Why?** He could draw before he could walk and completed his first painting at just 9 years old.

❖ **Fact:** Picasso's full name has 23 words! **Why?** His full name, *Pablo Diego José Francisco de Paula Juan Nepomuceno Crispín Crispiniano María Remedios de la Santísima Trinidad Ruiz Picasso*, honors various saints and relatives.

❖ **Fact:** Picasso co-founded the Cubist movement! **Why?** He and Georges Braque developed this style, which uses geometric shapes to depict subjects from multiple angles.

❖ **Fact:** Picasso created over 50,000 artworks! **Why?** He was incredibly prolific, producing paintings, drawings, sculptures, ceramics, prints, and more throughout his lifetime.

❖ **Fact:** Picasso's first word was "pencil"! **Why?** Growing up in an artistic family, he was surrounded by art supplies and began drawing at a very young age.

❖ **Fact:** Picasso's "Blue Period" was inspired by sadness! **Why?** After a friend's death, he painted in shades of blue and green to express his feelings of melancholy.

❖ **Fact:** Picasso's "Rose Period" was full of warmth! **Why?** During a happier time in his life, he used pinks and oranges to create more cheerful and romantic artworks.

❖ **Fact:** Picasso was also a playwright! **Why?** He wrote two plays, *Desire Caught by the Tail* and *The Four Little Girls*, showcasing his creativity beyond visual art.

❖ **Fact:** Picasso's art was influenced by African masks! **Why?** He admired their bold shapes and designs, which inspired some of his most famous works, like *Les Demoiselles d'Avignon*.

❖ **Fact:** Picasso's *Guernica* is a powerful anti-war statement! **Why?** This large mural depicts the horrors of war and was created in response to the bombing of the town of Guernica during the Spanish Civil War.

- ❖ **Fact:** Picasso was a master of reinvention! **Why?** He constantly experimented with different styles and techniques, never sticking to one way of creating art.

- ❖ **Fact:** Picasso's art is displayed in museums worldwide! **Why?** His influence on modern art is so significant that his works are featured in major museums, including the Louvre and the Museum of Modern Art.

- ❖ **Fact:** Picasso had a pet monkey! **Why?** He loved animals and often included them in his art, keeping a variety of pets throughout his life.

- ❖ **Fact:** Picasso's *The Weeping Woman* is a symbol of suffering! **Why?** This painting captures the pain and anguish of war, using distorted features to convey deep emotion.

- ❖ **Fact:** Picasso's legacy continues to inspire artists today! **Why?** His innovative approaches and groundbreaking styles have left a lasting impact on the art world, encouraging creativity and experimentation.

Alexander Hamilton

Born: 1757 – **Died:** 1804

Country/Region: United States (born in the Caribbean)

Known for: Founding Father, economist, first Secretary of the Treasury

Fun Fact: His life inspired a hit Broadway musical!

Alexander Hamilton was one of the most important architects of the United States. Born in the Caribbean and rising through hard work and intelligence, he helped write the U.S. Constitution, created the nation's financial system, and left a legacy that still shapes America today.

Fascinating Facts & Why They Matter

- ❖ **Fact:** Alexander Hamilton was one of the Founding Fathers of the United States!
  Why? He helped shape the new nation by writing many of the Federalist Papers, which supported the U.S. Constitution.

- ❖ **Fact:** Hamilton was the first Secretary of the Treasury!
  Why? He created the financial system that helped the United States pay off its debts and establish a national bank.

- ❖ **Fact:** Hamilton was born in the Caribbean!
  Why? He was born on the island of Nevis in 1755 or 1757, making him one of the few Founding Fathers not born in the American colonies.

- ❖ **Fact:** Hamilton was a self-taught lawyer!
  Why? He studied law on his own and passed the bar exam in New York, becoming a successful attorney.

- ❖ **Fact:** Hamilton founded the New York Post!
  Why? He started the newspaper in 1801 to share his political views and support the Federalist Party.

- ❖ **Fact:** Hamilton was a key figure in the creation of the U.S. Coast Guard!
  Why? He proposed the idea of a "Revenue Cutter Service" to enforce tariffs and prevent smuggling, which later became the Coast Guard.

- ❖ **Fact:** Hamilton's face is on the $10 bill!
  Why? He is honored for his significant contributions to the financial foundation of the United States.

- ❖ **Fact:** Hamilton was involved in a famous duel!
  Why? He was challenged by Aaron Burr, the Vice President, and was fatally wounded in 1804.

- ❖ **Fact:** Hamilton was an aide to George Washington during the Revolutionary War!
  Why? He served as Washington's right-hand man, helping with military strategies and correspondence.

- ❖ **Fact:** Hamilton was a strong advocate for a strong central government!
  Why? He believed that a powerful national government was necessary to maintain order and unity in the new country.

❖ **Fact:** Hamilton's life inspired a hit Broadway musical! **Why?** The musical *Hamilton* tells his story through hip-hop and other musical styles, making history fun and engaging.

❖ **Fact:** Hamilton helped establish the U.S. Mint! **Why?** He wanted to create a stable currency system, so he played a key role in founding the institution that produces American coins.

❖ **Fact:** Hamilton was a prolific writer! **Why?** He wrote over 51 of the 85 Federalist Papers, which argued for the ratification of the U.S. Constitution.

❖ **Fact:** Hamilton was a member of the Continental Congress! **Why?** He represented New York and worked on important issues like military funding and foreign relations.

❖ **Fact:** Hamilton's legacy continues to influence American politics! **Why?** His ideas about government and finance still shape discussions and policies today.

Jane Austen

Born: 1775 – **Died:** 1817
Country/Region: England
Known for: Novelist, author of *Pride and Prejudice*, *Emma*, and other beloved works
Fun Fact: Her face appears on the British £10 note!

📖 **Jane Austen was a brilliant English writer whose sharp wit and keen observations of society brought her characters to life. Writing during the Regency Era, she crafted novels filled with love, humor, and social commentary that remain some of the most cherished in English literature.**

Fascinating Facts & Why They Matter

❖ **Fact:** Jane Austen wrote her first novel at age 14! **Why?** She started writing *Love and Freindship* (yes, with that spelling) as a teenager, showcasing her early talent for storytelling.

❖ **Fact:** Austen's novels were published anonymously! **Why?** During her lifetime, her books were credited to "A Lady" because it was uncommon for women to publish under their own names.

❖ **Fact:** Jane Austen had seven siblings! **Why?** She was the seventh of eight children in her family, which gave her plenty of inspiration for the family dynamics in her novels.

❖ **Fact:** Austen's novels are set in the Regency Era! **Why?** This period, from 1811 to 1820, was known for its distinct social customs and fashion, which are vividly depicted in her stories.

❖ **Fact:** Jane Austen never married! **Why?** Although she received several marriage proposals, she chose to remain single and focus on her writing.

❖ **Fact:** Austen's novels have been adapted into over 70 films and TV shows!
Why? Her timeless stories and relatable characters continue to captivate audiences around the world.

❖ **Fact:** Jane Austen loved to dance!
Why? Dancing was a popular social activity in her time, and she often included lively dance scenes in her novels.

❖ **Fact:** Austen's writing desk was very small!
Why? She wrote her famous novels on a tiny, 12-sided table, showing that you don't need a big space to create great works.

❖ **Fact:** Jane Austen's face is on British currency!
Why? She is honored on the £10 note for her significant contributions to English literature.

❖ **Fact:** Austen's novels explore themes of love and social class!
Why? She used her keen observations of society to create stories that are both entertaining and thought-provoking.

❖ **Fact:** Jane Austen's letters provide insight into her life! **Why?** Her correspondence with family and friends reveals her wit, humor, and thoughts on her writing process.

❖ **Fact:** Austen's *Pride and Prejudice* was originally titled *First Impressions*!
Why? The novel's initial title reflected the misunderstandings and judgments between its main characters.

❖ **Fact:** Jane Austen's novels were not widely popular during her lifetime!
Why? Her works gained much more recognition and appreciation after her death, becoming classics of English literature.

❖ **Fact:** Austen's family supported her writing!
Why? Her father and brothers helped her publish her novels, recognizing her talent and encouraging her literary pursuits.

❖ **Fact:** Jane Austen's legacy continues to inspire readers and writers!
Why? Her sharp wit, memorable characters, and engaging plots have left a lasting impact on literature and popular culture.

Mahavira

Born: 599 BCE – **Died:** 527 BCE
Country/Region: Ancient India (modern-day Bihar)
Known for: Spiritual teacher, 24th Tirthankara of Jainism
Fun Fact: His symbol is the lion, representing fearlessness and royalty!

Mahavira was an Indian prince who gave up his royal life to seek spiritual truth. As the 24th Tirthankara of Jainism, he promoted a life of compassion, truth, and non-violence. His teachings became the foundation of Jain philosophy and continue to inspire peace and respect for all living beings.

Fascinating Facts & Why They Matter

❖ **Fact:** Mahavira was the 24th Tirthankara of Jainism! **Why?** He is considered a spiritual teacher who revived and reorganized the Jain religion in ancient India.

❖ **Fact:** Mahavira was born into a royal family! **Why?** He was born as Vardhamana in 599 BCE in the kingdom of Vaishali, which is now in modern-day Bihar, India.

❖ **Fact:** Mahavira renounced his royal life at age 30! **Why?** He left his home to seek spiritual awakening and spent 12 years as an ascetic, practicing intense meditation and self-discipline.

❖ **Fact:** Mahavira achieved *Kevala Jnana*, or omniscience! **Why?** After years of meditation and penance, he attained complete knowledge and enlightenment, becoming a *Kevalin*.

❖ **Fact:** Mahavira taught the principle of *Ahimsa*, or non-violence! **Why?** He believed in living a life of harmlessness and compassion toward all living beings, which is a core tenet of Jainism.

❖ **Fact:** Mahavira's teachings emphasized truth and honesty!
Why? He encouraged his followers to always speak the truth and live with integrity, which are key principles in Jain philosophy.

❖ **Fact:** Mahavira established the five great vows of Jainism!
Why? These vows—non-violence, truthfulness, non-stealing, celibacy, and non-possessiveness—guide Jains in their spiritual practice.

❖ **Fact:** Mahavira's followers are called Jains!
Why? The term "Jain" comes from the word *Jina*, meaning "conqueror," referring to those who conquer inner passions and desires.

❖ **Fact:** Mahavira's teachings were passed down orally!
Why? His disciples memorized and recited his teachings, which were later compiled into sacred texts known as *Agamas*.

❖ **Fact:** Mahavira attained *Nirvana* at the age of 72! **Why?** He passed away in 527 BCE, achieving liberation (*Moksha*) from the cycle of birth and death.

❖ **Fact:** Mahavira's life is celebrated during the festival of *Mahavir   Jayanti!* **Why?** This festival marks his birth and is one of the most important religious events for Jains, celebrated with prayers and processions.

❖ **Fact:**   Mahavira's   symbol   is   the   lion! **Why?** The lion represents his royal heritage and his fearless nature in spreading his teachings.

❖ **Fact:** Mahavira's teachings promote environmental awareness! **Why?** By advocating non-violence and respect for all life forms, his philosophy encourages the protection of nature and the environment.

❖ **Fact:** Mahavira's influence extends beyond Jainism! **Why?** His principles of non-violence and truth have inspired many, including Mahatma Gandhi, in their pursuit of peace and justice.

Louis Pasteur

Born: 1822 – **Died:** 1895
Country/Region: France
Known for: Developing vaccines, inventing pasteurization, founding microbiology
Fun Fact: He saved a young boy's life with the world's first rabies vaccine!

Louis Pasteur was a French scientist who changed the world with his discoveries about germs and disease. From inventing a safer way to drink milk to creating vaccines that saved lives, he helped lay the foundation for modern medicine and microbiology.

Fascinating Facts & Why They Matter

❖ **Fact:** Louis Pasteur discovered the principles of vaccination!
Why? He developed vaccines for diseases like rabies and anthrax, helping to prevent these illnesses in humans and animals.

❖ **Fact:** Pasteur invented pasteurization!
Why? This process involves heating liquids like milk to kill harmful bacteria, making them safer to drink.

❖ **Fact:** Louis Pasteur was a chemist and microbiologist!
Why? He studied tiny organisms and their effects on food and health, leading to groundbreaking discoveries in science.

❖ **Fact:** Pasteur proved that germs cause disease!
Why? He showed that microorganisms—not bad air or "miasma"—were responsible for infections, changing how we understand illness.

❖ **Fact:** Louis Pasteur saved the silk industry!
Why? He identified the cause of a disease affecting

silkworms and developed methods to prevent it, rescuing the industry from collapse.

❖ **Fact:** Pasteur's work led to the development of antiseptics!
Why? His discoveries about germs inspired doctors to use antiseptics to clean wounds and surgical tools, reducing infections.

❖ **Fact:** Louis Pasteur was born in France in 1822!
Why? He grew up in a small town called Dole, where he developed an early interest in science and nature.

❖ **Fact:** Pasteur's rabies vaccine saved a young boy's life!
Why? In 1885, he successfully treated a boy bitten by a rabid dog, proving the effectiveness of his vaccine.

❖ **Fact:** Louis Pasteur founded the Pasteur Institute!
Why? This research center, established in 1887, continues to study infectious diseases and develop new vaccines.

❖ **Fact:** Pasteur's discoveries laid the foundation for modern microbiology!
Why? His work on germs and disease prevention has had a lasting impact on medicine and public health.

❖ **Fact:** Louis Pasteur was awarded the Legion of Honor! **Why?** This prestigious French award recognized his significant contributions to science and society.

❖ **Fact:** Pasteur's experiments disproved spontaneous generation! **Why?** He showed that life does not arise from non-living matter, but from existing microorganisms.

❖ **Fact:** Louis Pasteur was a professor at the University of Strasbourg! **Why?** He taught chemistry and conducted research, sharing his knowledge with students and colleagues.

❖ **Fact:** Pasteur's work helped improve food safety! **Why?** By understanding how germs spoil food, he developed methods to preserve it longer and prevent illness.

❖ **Fact:** Louis Pasteur's legacy continues to inspire scientists! **Why?** His dedication to research and discovery has paved the way for countless advancements in health and science.

Sojourner Truth

Born: 1797 – **Died:** 1883
Country/Region: United States
Known for: Fighting for the end of slavery and for women's rights
Fun Fact: Her powerful speech, *"Ain't I a Woman?"*, is still quoted today!

🗣️ Sojourner Truth was a brave and determined woman who escaped slavery and became a powerful voice for justice. She traveled across the country speaking out against slavery and fighting for women's rights, inspiring generations with her fearless words and actions.

Fascinating Facts & Why They Matter

❖ **Fact:** Sojourner Truth was born into slavery in 1797! **Why?** She was born in Swartekill, New York, and given the name Isabella Baumfree.

❖ **Fact:** Sojourner Truth escaped to freedom in 1826! **Why?** She fled with her infant daughter, leaving behind her other children who were still enslaved.

❖ **Fact:** Sojourner Truth changed her name in 1843! **Why?** She believed God called her to travel and speak the truth, so she adopted the name Sojourner Truth.

❖ **Fact:** Sojourner Truth was an abolitionist and women's rights activist! **Why?** She dedicated her life to fighting for the end of slavery and for equal rights for women.

❖ **Fact:** Sojourner Truth delivered her famous *"Ain't I a Woman?"* speech in 1851! **Why?** She spoke at the Ohio Women's Rights Convention, challenging ideas about race and gender inequality.

- ❖ **Fact:** Sojourner Truth met President Abraham Lincoln in 1864!
  Why? She visited the White House to discuss her work and the condition of African Americans.

- ❖ **Fact:** Sojourner Truth helped recruit Black troops for the Union Army!
  Why? During the Civil War, she encouraged African American men to join the fight for freedom.

- ❖ **Fact:** Sojourner Truth was the first Black woman to win a court case against a white man!
  Why? She successfully sued for the return of her son, who had been illegally sold into slavery.

- ❖ **Fact:** Sojourner Truth worked to secure land grants for former slaves!
  Why? After the Civil War, she advocated for giving freed slaves land to help them build independent lives.

- ❖ **Fact:** Sojourner Truth's legacy continues to inspire!
  Why? Her courage, faith, and powerful words made her a lasting symbol of justice and equality.

Wolfgang Amadeus Mozart

Born: 1756 – **Died:** 1791
Country/Region: Austria
Known for: Writing beautiful and brilliant music
Fun Fact: He started composing when he was just five years old!

♫ Wolfgang Amadeus Mozart was a musical genius who amazed the world with his incredible talent from a young age. He wrote hundreds of pieces, including symphonies, operas, and sonatas, many of which are still performed and loved today. His music is full of creativity, emotion, and elegance that has stood the test of time.

Fascinating Facts & Why They Matter

❖ **Fact:** Wolfgang Amadeus Mozart composed over 600 pieces of music!
Why? He started composing at the age of five and continued throughout his life, creating a huge legacy of beautiful music.

❖ **Fact:** Mozart was a child prodigy!
Why? By age six, he was already performing for European royalty, showing his amazing talent on piano and violin.

❖ **Fact:** Mozart wrote his first symphony at the age of eight!
Why? His early start and natural gift for music helped him write complex pieces even as a child.

❖ **Fact:** Mozart could play multiple instruments!
Why? He mastered the piano, violin, and organ, which allowed him to compose in many different musical styles.

❖ **Fact:** Mozart's music is still popular today!
Why? His works are loved for their beauty, emotion, and technical brilliance, making them timeless.

❖ **Fact:** Mozart had perfect pitch!
Why? This rare talent helped him identify and play notes exactly by ear, boosting his musical abilities.

❖ **Fact:** Mozart's full name was Johannes Chrysostomus Wolfgangus Theophilus Mozart!
Why? It was common in his time to have many names, often honoring saints and family traditions.

❖ **Fact:** Mozart wrote his first opera at age 12!
Why? His early love for music and drama led him to compose operas that are still famous today.

❖ **Fact:** Mozart was born in Salzburg, Austria, in 1756!
Why? Salzburg was a musical city where he had many chances to learn and perform.

❖ **Fact:** Mozart's music influenced many composers!
Why? Great musicians like Beethoven admired him and learned from his style and creativity.

❖ **Fact:** Mozart's father was also a musician!
Why? Leopold Mozart supported his son's talent and took him on concert tours around Europe.

❖ **Fact:** Mozart's music includes famous operas like *The Magic Flute* and *Don Giovanni*!
   Why? These operas are loved for their fun stories and unforgettable music.

❖ **Fact:** Mozart's *Requiem* was unfinished at his death!
   Why? He died at just 35, and his student completed the powerful piece after he passed.

❖ **Fact:** Mozart's sister, Nannerl, was also a talented musician!
   Why? She performed with Mozart when they were children and was admired for her piano skills.

❖ **Fact:** Mozart's music is used in movies, commercials, and even video games!
   Why? His expressive and exciting music fits perfectly in all kinds of modern entertainment.

Charles Darwin

Born: 1809 – **Died:** 1882
Country/Region: England
Known for: Developing the theory of evolution by natural selection
Fun Fact: He got many of his ideas from observing birds and animals on a five-year sea voyage!

🐢 Charles Darwin was a scientist who changed the way we understand life on Earth. He loved exploring nature and studying plants and animals. His groundbreaking book, *On the Origin of Species*, explained how species change over time through a process called natural selection. His work laid the foundation for the science of biology and still influences how we think about the natural world today.

Fascinating Facts & Why They Matter

❖ **Fact:** Charles Darwin was born on February 12, 1809!
   Why? He was born in Shrewsbury, England, and grew up to become one of the most famous scientists in history.

❖ **Fact:** Darwin's most famous work is *On the Origin of Species*!
   Why? Published in 1859, this book introduced the theory of evolution by natural selection.

❖ **Fact:** Darwin traveled around the world on the HMS *Beagle*!
   Why? From 1831 to 1836, he explored many places and collected samples that helped shape his scientific ideas.

❖ **Fact:** Darwin studied finches on the Galápagos Islands!
   Why? He noticed their beaks were different depending on what they ate, helping him understand how animals adapt to their environment.

❖ **Fact:** Darwin was a naturalist!
   Why? He loved observing nature, and his careful studies led to new ideas about how species change over time.

❖ **Fact:** Darwin's theory of evolution was controversial! **Why?** It challenged traditional beliefs about how life began and developed, leading to debate and discussion.

❖ **Fact:** Darwin was inspired by other scientists! **Why?** He read books by geologists and economists, which helped him think about change, survival, and nature.

❖ **Fact:** Darwin married his cousin, Emma Wedgwood! **Why?** They had ten children and shared a love of learning, science, and family life.

❖ **Fact:** Darwin was a member of the Royal Society! **Why?** This respected group of scientists honored him for his important work in biology and evolution.

❖ **Fact:** Darwin's work laid the foundation for modern biology! **Why?** His theory of evolution is still used today to understand the diversity of life on Earth.

❖ **Fact:** Darwin was buried in Westminster Abbey! **Why?** He was given this great honor because of his lasting impact on science and the world.

Conclusion

For Parents, Teachers, and Grown-Ups

As you've explored these pages, you've met a remarkable variety of people — scientists, artists, leaders, inventors, writers, and brave changemakers. They came from different times, different places, and different backgrounds. But they all shared something powerful: **they lived with purpose, and they left a mark**.

This book is more than a collection of facts. It's a journey through values — the kind of values that help children grow into thoughtful, curious, and kind human beings.

In every story, there is something to admire and to reflect on:

- **Courage**, like Anne Frank's or Nelson Mandela's.

- **Curiosity**, like Galileo's or Marie Curie's.

- **Creativity**, like Frida Kahlo's or Beethoven's.

- **Determination**, like Helen Keller's or Susan B. Anthony's.

- **Empathy and justice**, like Sojourner Truth's or Mother Teresa's.

These are values that speak not only to history, but to **the future** — to the children who will grow up reading these stories and asking questions about the world.

Whether you're a parent, a teacher, or a caregiver, we hope this book has sparked not just wonder, but also meaningful conversations. Every child has their own gifts. And every child can be inspired to use them for good.

Because the real heroes of tomorrow might be the ones reading this book today.

www.ingramcontent.com/pod-product-compliance
Lightning Source LLC
Chambersburg PA
CBHW060853280326
41934CB00007B/1033